The Mochica

Art and Civilization of Indian America
General Editor Dr. Michael Coe

with 144 illustrations, 7 in colour

Elizabeth P. Benson

The Mochica

A Culture of Peru

Thames and Hudson · London

First published in Great Britain in 1972 by
Thames and Hudson Ltd, London
Published in the U.S.A. by
Praeger Publishers Inc., New York

Printed in Great Britain

ISBN 0 500 72001 0

Contents

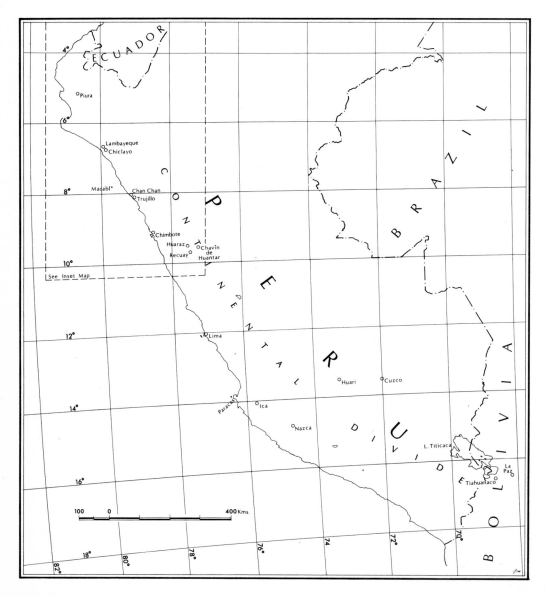

Peru

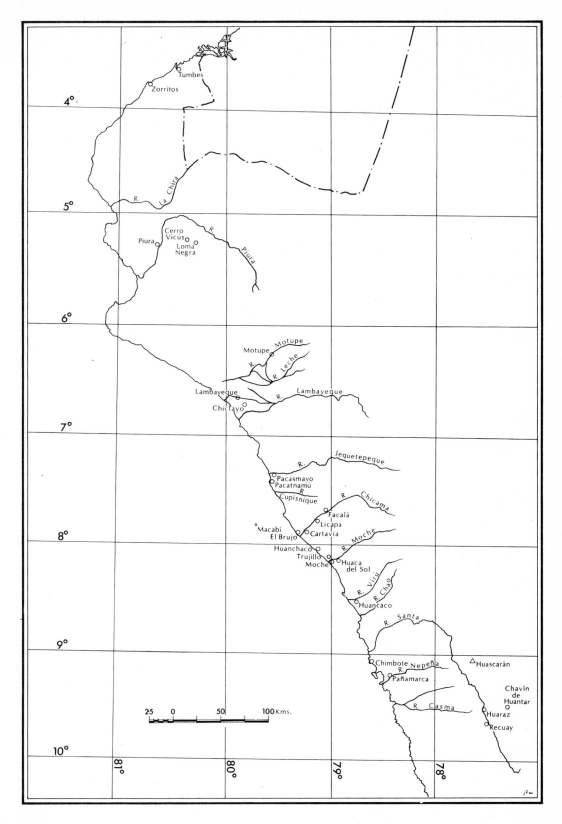

The Mochica Area

Acknowledgments

I am grateful to Michael D. Coe, Geoffrey Bushnell, Paul H. Gebhard, Thomas C. Patterson, Victor Antonio Rodriguez Suy Suy, and Allen Wardwell, who offered me their time and ideas; to Margarita and Alex Ciurlizza, Oscar Fernández de Córdova, Guillermo Ganoza, and André Garde de Ste. Croix, who extended their hospitality to me; to Ingeborg Bolz of the Rautenstrauch-Joest Museum, Gunnar Didrichsen of the Didrichsen Art Museum, and H. Friedrich of the Bremen Übersee-Museum, who supplied me with photographs; to Richard Amt, who produced the Dumbarton Oaks photographs; to John Wilson, who contributed the maps; to Isham Perkins and to all those others at Dumbarton Oaks who gave me their support and cooperation and the use of the facilities there, and especially to Barbara Braun, who played the perfect sounding-board.

ELIZABETH P. BENSON

Washington D.C.,
June, 1971

Introduction

If one mentions pre-Columbian Peru, the response will most often be "Oh, yes, the Inca." But the Inca were latecomers and short-stayers at the end of a long and complex succession of interacting civilizations. For two and a half millenniums before the Inca, people had been farming, weaving cloth, worshiping in impressive structures, making elaborate ceremonial pottery, and working metal. Peru was the hub of the central Andean area where some of the highest cultures of the New World developed, comparable only to those that evolved in Mexico and its adjacent areas. The common divisions of Peruvian archaeology are made between the highlands and the coastal lowlands, and these in turn are divided into northern, central, and southern areas. Religions and art styles, usually inextricably related, often moved from one area to another and in the process were somewhat transformed by the patterns of the different regions, by climate and raw materials, by local history and tradition.

The most fascinating of the north-coast cultures and one of the most provocative in Peruvian prehistory is that of the Mochica, who left one of the richest legacies of artifacts in all the Andes. Historically, nothing is known of the Mochica, for several waves of conquest in the north separated them from the Inca, whose era has provided our only direct knowledge of pre-Spanish Peruvian peoples. What is known of the Mochica is the wealth of their decorated pottery, as well as other artifacts and architecture. This book makes certain conjectures about the way of life of the Mochica, using Mochica remains for clues to their beliefs and customs. Interpretations that seem relatively safe now may be proved wrong in the future with further knowledge, but one must begin to posit those interpretations.

Mochica remains have been found from the Piura Valley, near the Ecuadorian border, down to the Nepeña Valley, some 249 miles north of Lima. The Mochica inhabited these northern valleys in the Early Intermediate Period, a span of time running from late in the last millennium before Christ through most of the first millennium after Christ. Carbon-14 dates for the area and period are scarce, but the following have been published:

9

★ *This date is*
extraordinarily early.

C-382	(Chicago) Huaca del Sol, Moche	873 ± 500 B.C.★
C-619	(Chicago) Huaca de la Cruz, Virú Valley; cord from a late Mochica burial	A.D. 33 ± 190
L-335a	(Lamont) Huaca de la Cruz, Virú Valley; textile fragment	A.D. 656 ± 80
L-335b	(Lamont) Huaca de la Cruz, Virú Valley; basket fragment	A.D. 656 ± 80

Heinrich Ubbelohde-Doering reports a Heidelberg University carbon-14 date from Pacatnamú of A.D. 485 ± 100, and George Kubler has produced a date of A.D. 850 from his guano study. The beginning of the Mochica period probably dates from just before the Christian era, and the end is probably dated in the early or mid-eighth century. Some of the recently published dates for the whole span of Mochica civilization are as follows:

Disselhoff (1967)   A.D. 0–800
Lanning (1967)   A.D. 200–600
Sawyer (1968)   300 B.C.–A.D. 700
Rowe   AD 1 — 600+

More carbon-14 dates are needed before the chronology can be firmly fixed.

The civilization is also called Moche, Pre-Chimú, Early Chimú, and Proto-Chimú, the Chimú being later people who dominated this area just before the expansion of the Inca Empire. The term "Mochica," which comes from the language spoken in this area until fairly recently and from the name of the Moche River, which flows through the valley containing the major Mochica remains, has been chosen for use here in preference to the often used "Moche" because "Mochica" is adjectival and implies a broader geographical range than the term that refers only to the river, valley, and village of Moche. The greatest development took place in the Moche Valley (also called the Santa Catalina Valley) and the Chicama Valley, a considerably larger valley just to the north. Somewhat after its establishment in these two valleys, the style appeared farther to the south, in the architecture and pottery of the Virú Valley. In the next three valleys southward, there is also evidence of the Mochica presence. The Chao Valley is small; the Santa Valley has yielded a great quantity of Mochica pottery, and, in the Nepeña Valley, apparently the southern limit of the Mochica domain, there is an impressive ceremonial center but little in the way of house remains. This southernmost outpost seems to have been conquered but not seriously colonized. It is possible, of course, that it was only the religious cult that spread, without political power. However, the military activity depicted on their artifacts suggests that the Mochica were people who converted by means of military force and secular conquest.

Evidence of the Mochica also appears in the valleys to the north of the Moche-Chicama heartland. There was a Mochica occupation in the Jequetepeque Valley, and pottery of Mochica style has been found in the Lambayeque-Leche-Motupe river complex. It was thought that the Mochica presence in the north was fairly slight, however, until recently, when a considerable amount of material of early Mochica style was found in the Piura Valley, first at Cerro Vicús and later at Loma Negra.

The Mochica produced hundreds of magnificent artifacts admired by travelers since the sixteenth century and, since the nineteenth century, highly desirable to collectors. The great collections now in the Berlin Museum, for example, date well back into the nineteenth century. In the late nineteenth century, E. G. Squier and E. W. Middendorf published observations on the Mochica. In 1902–3, Arthur Baessler published in four folio volumes—three of which are almost entirely concerned with Mochica pottery—his own Peruvian collection, now in the Berlin Museum, with drawings by Wilhelm von den Steinen.

Archaeological study in the area has been of varying intensity, so that some regions have been studied thoroughly and some only very slightly. Organized archaeology in the area began at the turn of the century, with Max Uhle's excavations, for the University of California, in the Moche Valley, where he worked at the Huaca del Sol and the Huaca de la Luna. Uhle's work was followed up by A. L. Kroeber, for the Field Museum, in the 1920's. Rafael Larco Hoyle worked extensively in the Chicama Valley and formed what is probably the greatest collection of Mochica pottery in the world, now housed in the Musèo Larco Herrera in Lima. He also published extensively and established a seriation for Mochica pottery. Wendell Bennett worked in the Chicama Valley and in the Virú and Lambayeque valleys.

One of the most thorough archaeological projects ever undertaken in Peru was the Virú Valley program. The Virú is a small valley, but one in which all the known strata of pre-Columbian occupation for the north coast are represented. Prior to the Virú Valley program, Kroeber, Bennett, and Larco had surveyed the Virú Valley. The Virú Valley program was set up by Wendell Bennett of Yale University, William Duncan Strong of Columbia University, Julian H. Steward of the Institute of Social Anthropology of the Smithsonian Institution, and Gordon R. Willey of the Bureau of American Ethnology of the Smithsonian Institution. Other archaeologists who became involved in this program were Junius Bird of the American Museum of Natural History, James A. Ford of Columbia University and the American Museum of Natural History, Clifford Evans, Jr., of Columbia University, and Donald Collier of the Natural History Museum in Chicago. This project resulted in a number of publications that form the basis of most of our information about the area.

More recent work has included that of Ubbelohde-Doering, who worked in the Jequetepeque Valley at various times between 1931 and 1964; Richard P. Schaedel, who worked, with the Institute of

Anthropology of the University of Trujillo, at Pañamarca in the Nepeña Valley; and Gerdt Kutscher of the Ibero-Amerikanische Institut in Berlin, who has written works on Mochica iconography, using some of the Von den Steinen drawings not published by Baessler, as well as other picture sources, for a rich presentation of visual material. Also useful in Mochica studies are the anthropological observations made by John Gillin in the 1940's in the village of Moche, where he found crafts and conventions inherited from Mochica ancestors of nearly two millenniums ago, as well as the studies made by Horst Nachtigall of fishing life on the north coast, and the work of Paul Kosok. Presently, research on Mochica iconography is being carried out by Christopher Donnan at the University of California, Los Angeles.

Chapter one   **The Rivers, The Sea, And The Desert**

The coast of Peru is one of the driest deserts in the world. A narrow strip of sand lies between the vast expanse of the Pacific Ocean and the Andes that rise steeply to snow-capped peaks within a few miles of the coast. The moist trade winds that blow from the east across the Amazon Basin deposit their moisture on the eastern mountains so that the western slopes of the Andes are dry and barren. The cold Humboldt Current, flowing parallel to the Peruvian coast, causes the humid sea winds to condense offshore, so that when these winds reach the land they are dry, picking up moisture from the shore rather than depositing it. Rain along the coast is rare, although every seven to twenty-five years there may be a deluge caused by a shifting of the track of the Humboldt Current. Normally, the coast has an annual precipitation of 0·2 inch; most of this moisture comes from fog. Because of the current and its winds, the coastal climate is relatively cool, in spite of its closeness to the Equator. The sand of the desert is blown by the winds into sculptural forms; the color of the sand varies from white to tan to rosy pink; scrub growth sometimes dots its paleness. The desert is impressively various, but the landscape is always stark, and the hills and mountains that rise from the sands are also bare.

In spots, the coastal desert is crossed by rivers coming down from the mountains. Here water permits irrigation and cultivation, and the desert is suddenly slashed by slices of green (*Color Plate I*). Since ancient times, these river valleys have been populated and cultivated by successive groups of people. The Mochica civilization came toward the middle of the whole development, at a time when technical advances allowed agriculturalists and craftsmen a wide range of activity yet before populations grew larger and art styles became stereotyped by mass production, as they did in later periods in Peru before the Spanish Conquest.

A millennium or so before the Mochica, the dominant civilization in the north of Peru was one called Chavín; it was the first major Andean civilization. Its center, as far as we know today, was the ceremonial site at the village of Chavín de Huantar, over the mountains, on the eastern slopes of the Andes. Here, as early as 1100 or

1-1. A stirrup-spout pot representing the head of the Chavín staff god, with feline fangs and a mouth ending in an arrow shape. The eye is more rectangular than round, with the iris at the top. Height, 8½ inches.

1500

1200 B.C., people began to build a masonry structure—with rooms, galleries, ramps, and air-vents—that was richly decorated with sculpture, most of which is incised or in low relief. They also made complex pottery (*Ill. 1–1*) and worked metal (*Ill. 1–2*). The themes of Chavín art consist mostly of creatures who combine the attributes of various animals—the feline, the eagle, the snake—with human attributes (*Ill. 1–3*). Whether this civilization originated at Chavín itself or elsewhere in the Andes—down in the Amazon Basin or on the Pacific coast—is still an unsolved problem. In any case, its most dramatic manifestation is at Chavín de Huantar, and its stylistic influence spread far afield, reaching southward at least as far as the southern Peruvian coast on the Paracas peninsula below Lima. It spread to, among other places, the northern coastal valleys, the general area later inhabited by the Mochica, where the Chavín style is known as Coastal Chavín or Cupisnique, after the Cupisnique *quebrada* (gorge), where many artifacts of this style have been found.

The tradition of working large stones did not come down to the coast—there is virtually no stone-carving on the coast from any period—but the style did come in pottery and metalworking.

The Chavín style was one of the components of the Mochica style. There was a period of Mochica development when there was a conscious archaizing that yielded pots with designs that clearly imitate Chavín. But many Chavín-derived motifs were always deeply ingrained in Mochica art and thought—a deity, for example, with a snake belt and double fangs in a mouth with arrow ends, as well as a number of lesser motifs. Whether the Chavín heritage was found on the spot in the coastal valleys, whether it had been transmitted through other people, or whether the Mochica actually knew about the site at Chavín de Huantar, we do not know. There probably was some combination of these possibilities.

Mochica art also was related to that of other north-coast groups, the most important relationship being that with the recently discovered finds in the area of Cerro Vicús in the Piura Valley of northernmost Peru. Here several styles have been found, among them modeled pots of extraordinarily fine quality—kneeling human figures, effigy birds (*Ill. 1–5*), and animals—of pure early Mochica

1–2. A hammered gold pendant disk, with a stylized face of the Chavín smiling god. A pair of snakes issues from the bottom of the mouth. Height, $4\frac{7}{8}$ inches.

1–3. A carved stone cup of Chavín style, decorated with a creature who has a stylized human body with a feline head and the wings and beak of an eagle. He holds a snake head in a taloned hand. At the top of the wing is a step-and-wave motif.

style, as well as objects of gold, silver, and copper (*Ill. 1–4*) with Mochica motifs. Many of the themes are identical with those of early Mochica pottery from the Mochica heartland; a few often repeated themes seem to be peculiar to the Vicús area. The identifiably close connection between Mochica and Vicús has not yet been defined. Thus far, only graves, not architecture, have been found in this northernmost region. It is possible that the Mochica style first developed somewhere in an unexplored region between the Piura and Chicama valleys or even in the Piura region itself. There are presently gaps in our archaeological knowledge that need to be filled to find answers to questions about the sources and early development of Mochica civilization.

Preceding the Mochica on their own ground were the civilization called Salinar, in the Chicama Valley, and then the Gallinazo, or Virú, the main development of which was in the Virú Valley (these styles also appeared as far north as the Piura Valley). Salinar pottery is white on red, with pots often modeled in simplified human and animal forms with a stirrup spout. Gallinazo pottery was decorated with negative painting; the effigy pots often portrayed the same subject matter that appeared on later Mochica wares (*Ills. 1–6 and 1–7*). Gallinazo architectural concepts were also the close predecessors of those of the Mochica. The Gallinazo style lasted in the Virú Valley until well after the Mochica culture had developed in the Chicama and Moche valleys.

1–4. A small copper mask with shell inlay in the eyes and mouth. A deity face from Loma Negra, near Piura, that strongly reflects the Chavín source. Height, $3\frac{3}{8}$ inches.

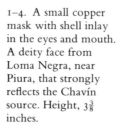

1–5. A stirrup-spout pot in the form of an owl, from the Vicús region in northern Peru. The owl stands like a man, with human legs and what appears to be a loincloth. Height, 8¼ inches.

1–6. A Gallinazo double "whistling" vessel depicting a macaw. When liquid moves in the vessel, air comes through the holes and makes a whistling sound. Height, 5¾ inches.

1–7. A Mochica double "whistling" vessel. This is a rather rare late Mochica survival of the Gallinazo form. The double whistling jar was a type of pre-Columbian pottery that existed from Mexico down through Peru. Height, 6¾ inches.

1–8. A Recuay pot with a figure whose ear ornaments and sunrise fan headdress are like those on Mochica figures. The "monster-in-the-moon" depicted on the shirt is also a Mochica motif.

In the mountains, another style contemporary with the Mochica was that usually called Recuay, after a town in the Callejón de Huaylas, a long valley lying between the two main cordilleras of the Andes, not far from Chavín de Huantar. The style has sometimes been called Huaylas or Santa (after the Santa River, which flows through the Callejón). The ceramics of Recuay are quite distinct from those of the Mochica—they are decorated with a red slip and negative painting and represent wooden-faced figures with popping eyes—but a number of the same motifs and scenes appear (*Ill. 1–8*).

During the Mochica centuries, the inhabitants of the coastal valleys would have been exposed to many styles and ideas in the course of trade and conquest. Different motifs come and go at different periods of Mochica history. Similarities with, say. Recuay may not have been so much a matter of influence as of common heritage.

19

1–9. Three Chimú pots. The stirrup spout with the small figure, at the left, is characteristic of Chimú ceramics, as are the "stippled" design on the other two pots and the simplified face of the pot at the right.

Following the Mochica civilization, there was a brief period of Tiahuanaco-Huari influence. The Tiahuanaco-Huari style spread up the coast, undoubtedly by conquest, from the southern highlands of Peru and Bolivia, and briefly influenced the north coast. The late style of the far north coast is usually called Lambayeque, related to Mochica, Tiahuanaco, and the succeeding Chimú. About A.D. 1000, the Chimú conquered a territory larger than that of the Mochica and dominated what had been the Mochica area. As the Mochica had sometimes archaized with Chavín-type pottery, so the Chimú made pots that clearly revived many Mochica forms (*Ill. 1–9*). Indeed, there are similarities so close that many people have felt that there was actually a continuity that was not totally disrupted by the Tiahuanaco-Huari spread. But, although shapes and motifs are often very similar (stirrup-spout pots of human figures, animals, fruits, or even the Mochica deity), the spirit behind Chimú art is very different. The ideas are more limited, the creative variety of Mochica pottery is missing, and the pots look mass-produced. The last pre-Conquest occupation of the area was, of course, the pan-Peruvian civilization of the Inca, which was, in social and economic terms, one of the most highly organized societies in the history of the world. Originating in the southern highlands of Peru, it spread up into Ecuador and down into Chile and Argentina, over a distance of some 2,500 miles of varied terrain and climate.

The main elements of Mochica life were the sea, the vegetation grown in the valleys, the desert sand, and the mountains (*Ill. 1–10*). The products and creatures of this sharply varied environment dominate Mochica art motifs and are reflected in ritual life. These were positive and negative elements, all of which had to be coped with, all of which had power and influence in daily activities. The sea and the cultivated valleys provided a livelihood that required constant effort. The desert was an enemy to be overcome, and the sea, too, had to be fought to gain sustenance. The mountains constituted a barrier to trading, for they and the forest lands on the other side produced objects for daily life as well as for ritual purposes.

Because of the lack of rainfall, there was a need for irrigation, which began in pre-Mochica times, and was further developed by the Mochica and later by the Chimú. Ancient abandoned canals give evidence of a wide system of waterworks. Today, the irrigated valleys of the north are green with crops of sugar-cane, corn, potatoes, cotton, rice, peanuts, and peppers. Although the crops are now somewhat different, the landscape in Mochica times must have looked much the same.

As in the past, the sea provides one of the richest fishing grounds in the world. The Humboldt Current, which sweeps up from the Antarctic, flows just off this coast, carrying with it plankton and abundant fish. The sea, then as now, provided not only fish but also seals, sea-lions, birds, salt-water shrimps, crabs, and edible seaweed. Mochica fishermen went to sea in rafts made of bundles of totora reeds; similar rafts are still made on the Mochica coast.

The mountains close off the view to the east and almost crowd the narrow strip of coastal lowland into the sea. Indeed, sometimes the hills plunge directly down into the sea, the present-day road clinging to their edges or going behind them. And yet the valleys and passes into these mountains were traversed by the Mochica, as they had been for centuries before. The more one learns of history, the more one realizes that people have always traveled, no matter how difficult the obstacles of the terrain.

I–IO. A view of the Moche Valley from the Huaca del Sol. The Moche River passes through the trees in the foreground. Cows graze to the right, fields of sugar cane are shown in the middle ground, and the sandy foothills of the Andes are in the background.

1–11. Effigy pot in the form of potatoes. Such realistic representations of fruits and vegetables are common in Mochica pottery.

The Mochica were clearly a warlike people. They not only fought the sea, the dry desert, and the wild, steep mountains, but they also fought for new land to cultivate, acquiring additional territory through conquest. They conquered foreign tribes and perhaps even fought among themselves. The warriors carried large clubs and square or round shields (*Ill. 1–15*), and they used slings and spear-throwers. They did not kill their enemies in battle, but took them prisoner and led them triumphantly back, probably to be sacrificed.

However, in spite of their concentration on warlike activities and on winning a livelihood, the Mochica had the time, energy, skill, and taste to erect large pyramids and buildings and to adorn them with mural paintings. They had the most advanced metallurgy in Peru at the time. They made headdresses of gold and masks of copper, they worked silver and gilded it, and they carved figures and implements from wood, inlaying them with turquoise and shell.

Numerous artifacts from their civilization still exist, but the most important remains are their pottery vessels—some of the handsomest and most informative in the world. One could illustrate a guide to the flora and fauna of the north of Peru using Mochica pots, which show varieties of birds (*Ill. 1–14*), fish (*Ill. 1–13*), frogs, lizards, llamas, jaguars, and pumas (*Ills. 1–12 and 1–17*) as well as fruits and vegetables—corn, squash, peppers, and potatoes (*Ill. 1–11*)—and cacti, trees, and other plants. The Mochica left behind portraits of

1-12. A detail of a Mochica pot in the form of a puma, or mountain lion.

1-13. An effigy lobster vessel, with an opening in the top. Length, 15 inches.

1–14. An effigy vessel of a sea bird. Height, 8¾ inches.

their chieftains (*Ill. 1–16*), representations of people who were diseased or deformed, scenes showing warriors in battle, rituals, processions with musicians, fishing, the hunting of deer and seals (*Ill. 1–18*), along with pictures of boats and houses, marshes and deserts. There is no problem with the immediate interpretation of these things, for they are all rendered with a wonderful realism. But the Mochica mind did not always concern itself with what we consider realistic representations, and the artifacts do not merely record daily life. A pot in the shape of a squash has a neck that turns into a bird's head. Warriors may have wings and the beaks of hummingbirds or hawks. A human face appears on a potato. Beans have legs and faces and carry weapons. To the Mochica, these were probably as real as the simple squash or frog or deer, and perhaps more meaningful, although the simpler forms must also have been charged with meaning. One has to be very careful in speaking of Mochica realism or in stating, "They left us a wonderful record of their daily life." Anything one says about Mochica religious life is a guess, but it is certain that all their artifacts had significance in terms of powerful chieftains, agricultural fertility, sea fertility, and the appeasement of deities or demons. The Mochica artist did not realistically represent the squash and the llama simply to show what their plants and animals looked like; there was surely some magic, religious, or symbolic reason for these representations.

1–15. A box made of six pieces of
steatite tied together. The wide sides
of the box have incised designs depicting warriors with clubs confronting
each other. On each short side is a
single warrior. Height, 2¼ inches.

1–16. A portrait of a Mochica chieftain with a water lily on his headdress. Height,
12 inches.

1–17. The head of a puma wearing a man's headdress and the face paint used by
Mochica dignitaries. Height, 12½ inches.

One must be careful with the ethnographic realities of remote peoples, careful in the interpretation of pictures of myth and belief. In the twentieth century, we make clear distinctions between what we consider real and what we consider fantasy, but to people in other eras our fantasy may be a reality and our reality may be charged with a magical significance of which we would not dream. The task of looking back over approximately two millenniums to reconstruct the thinking of a people is fraught with problems that are compounded by the fact that the Mochica, like all Andean people, had no writing. Probably no other people in the history of the world—with the possible exception of the Greeks—have told us as much about themselves on their pottery as did the Mochica. Their beliefs are surely all described there; the problem lies in the interpretation of this information. For the Greeks also left us written material, but the Mochica did not. Because they were not literate, their iconography was particularly important. The artistic motifs are meaningful symbols that substituted in a sense for writing. The constantly repeated symbols—the step, the stepped square, the stripe, the wave, the **S**, the angular **S**, the checkerboard pattern, the dark-and-light alteration, and so on—must have been used to communicate ideas. Recurring figures—a bearded man wearing a cape and sea symbols, a pale man with strange face paint, and other figures who appear again and again—must have been characters in folklore, and each deity and demon must have had both attributes and a history, which were revealed in their representations.

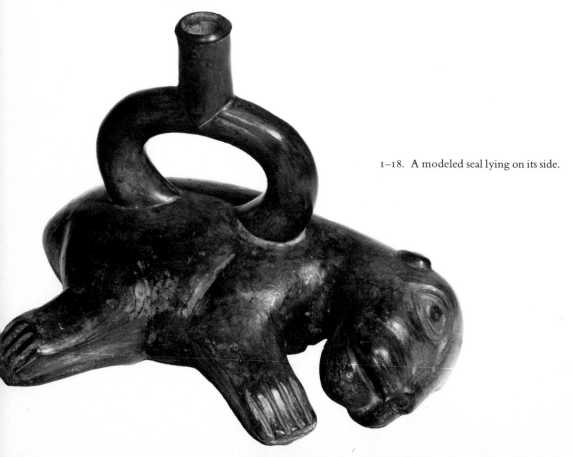

1–18. A modeled seal lying on its side.

Chapter two　　　**The God Who Came Down From The Mountains**

The supreme deity of the Mochica dwelt in the mountains. He is
represented sitting on a platform or throne, surrounded by mountain
peaks, beside a scene of great activity, from which he is set apart
(*Ill. 2–1*). Not human, not involved, but rather as massive and im-
mobile as a sculptured monument, he faces straight ahead, with the
round, staring eyes and double fangs of a feline set in an angular
mouth; his scale is larger than that of the participants in the action. He
usually wears a semicircular "sunrise" headdress with a jaguar head
on the front, snake-head ear ornaments, and an enveloping cloak or
robe; he sits with his hands on his knees. In other representations, he
appears seated in the form of a "mountain" pot, with the peaks seeming to emerge from his body, as if he himself were the mountain.
In such cases, he is usually flanked by two snakes. Other pots represent
only the head of the deity, with bulging eyes and snake-head ear
ornaments. This *deus otiosus*, remote from the affairs of men, impassive
and impressive, was probably a creator god, deriving from the old
Chavín deities of the great temple in the mountains. The Mochica
pottery representations may actually depict a sky god, the mountains
being the closest thing to the sky that could be represented. Because
the Andes are some of the highest mountains in the world, this is not a
naïve idea. Huascarán, the highest mountain in Peru—over 22,000
feet—is not far from Chavín de Huantar.

More frequently represented than the creator god is a deity with
essentially the same attributes: He has the Chavín feline mouth, snake-
head earrings, and a jaguar or sunrise headdress. He commonly has
one or two snakes extending from his belt and is most often pictured
wearing trunks and a shirt with a step motif. His ear ornaments are
either snake heads, large round spools or pendants, or a figure eight.
This second deity, unlike the first, is always shown as an active figure,
usually in profile, and with legs and arms in motion. Whether he is in
fact an active manifestation of the supreme deity, an offspring, or a
divine representation from the supreme god to the Mochica people
is open to question; yet he is certainly something of this sort. He is
god-the-son, who came down to the coast from the mountains—
perhaps from Chavín itself. He is predominantly the god of the coast,

27

2–1. A mountain sacrifice scene, with the deity seated at the left and two victims, one with streaming hair on the centre peak, and one lying nude below.

whereas god-the-father is the god of the mountains (or sky), although both have associations with the mountains and the sea as well. At least two pots represent a scene in the mountains in which the creator god is shown in a cave with a large snake at either side of his head, while the active deity stands poised at the side (*Ill. 2–2*).

This deity (*Ill. 2–3*), who has generally not been subdivided as he is here, is sometimes called Ai Apaec, the Chimú name for the later version of the god; he has also been called the "god of the snake extension," this extension of his belt being perhaps the most consistent attribute of the deity, although he might just as well be called the "god of the snake earring." It is probably most satisfactory to call the active deity the "fanged god," because the feline essence is probably most powerful, and the passive deity the "creator god" or "supreme deity." These deities always have the double fangs or a Chavinoid mouth or both, although double fangs are not reserved strictly for them but are probably a sign of divinity or supernatural power in general (*Color Plate II*). Sometimes it is difficult to tell which of the two deities is represented. Usually, however, the creator god is shown frontally and symmetrically, wearing a sunrise headdress and staring off into space, whereas the active god is in profile, has knees bent in action, wears trunks rather than a long garment, and wears a simple jaguar headdress rather than the sunrise version.

Unlike the supreme deity, the fanged god is concerned—on certain levels, at least—with the affairs of man, particularly coastal man. Like Quetzalcóatl in Mexico, this deity was probably anachronistically given credit for the introduction of earlier inventions and discoveries. It is likely that he was thought to have introduced maize (which appeared on the coast at the time the Chavín style arrived there), since there are frequent representations of maize and other vegetables with the head of the creator god emerging from them

2–2. The creator god, with sunrise headdress, in a mountain cave, flanked by large snakes. The fanged god, in jaguar headdress, stands at the left, with his snake belt curving below him.

2–3. The deity standing and holding a conch shell. He has round eyes, a sunrise headdress with a jaguar head and paws, and snake earrings.

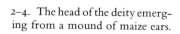
2–4. The head of the deity emerging from a mound of maize ears.

(*Ill.* *2–4*). (It is interesting, however, that the active god is rarely depicted in a context of agricultural activity.) As the god who came down from the mountains, he may well be the deity of fresh water, of the rivers that also come down from the mountains; fresh water, making possible the cultivation of the valleys, was, of course, the life blood of Mochica civilization.

The fanged god may also be—or, more likely, may represent—the sun, since the sun rises every day from the mountains. The creator god may actually be the sun who sends this moving manifestation down to the coast daily. The ethnographic literature of South America is full of references to a creator god, or a supreme god, who is the sun, as well as to a deity who sends his body out from himself. There are several painted representations of the head of the deity—without a body—represented as a circular face with rays emanating from it (*Ill.* *2–5*). Other possible evidence for the concept of the deity as a sun god is that both the active and passive types are generally represented with round, staring, birdlike eyes, suggesting the globe of the sun. The sun has a recurring contest with the sea, as each day it comes from the mountains, battles the sea, and wins because, although it sinks into the sea, it always reappears. The Mochica fishermen went to sea at night and hopefully conquered the sea, returning safely the next day, so they might naturally think of a sun god who did the same thing.

Although at times the deity seems to be represented as a sea god, he is essentially the deity of the people who live on the coast, protecting them from sea monsters and helping them win a livelihood from the sea. Such a concept of a deity is appropriate for a fishing people. The fanged god is the super-Mochica. He goes to sea in a raft (*Ill.* *2–6*) and catches fish as Mochica fishermen must have done; he decapitates or cuts the throats of seabirds. He hunts deer with a spear (and was probably the patron of hunters), but he is most frequently seen in contests—which he always wins—with demons of the sea. His real adversaries are monsters from the deep, whom he confronts with a knife that usually has a snake head or a bird head tied by a string to the handle. The deity often appears with a wrinkled face that perhaps does not suggest age so much as a long submersion in the sea (*Ill.* *2–18*).

There are certain classic encounters of the fanged god: Most frequently represented are those with a fish monster and a crab monster (*Ills.* *2–16 and 2–17*). Sometimes the fish monster has a human head and clothing; most often it is a fish with a human leg, a human arm, and a hand that characteristically holds a knife. The fish monster has serrated edges along its fins (this serration is a common Mochica motif, possibly deriving from sharks' teeth). The crab monster is puzzling, because it frequently seems to be a kind of *alter ego* of the fanged god, with feline fangs of its own. It is often marked with a fanged face on its shell. The crab monster may have been an ancient sea deity, and the face on the shell may be an indication of its conquest by the Mochica god. The picture is further complicated by the fact that the deity himself sometimes appears in a crab form when he is

2–5. A dipper, or "corn-popper," with the round head of the deity with painted face.

2–6. The fanged god in a raft, with the fish monster on the end of a line. The raft has a monster head on each end and seems to be supported by an anthropomorphic cormorant.

fighting the fish monster (*Ills. 2–7 and 2–22*). The deity apparently had the ability to change form when necessary: He occasionally has the body of a dragonfly (when killing a seabird) or that of a fresh-water shrimp.

It is possible, of course, that what has been described here as a single or double deity is actually many deities, but the repetition of scenes and of details of dress and attributes argues against this. It is also possible that the figures on pottery may represent priests imitating the deity, but, although this may well have been a Mochica religious activity, it is likely that the pottery depicts the deity himself. On occasion, a figure with a fanged Chavinoid mouth and snake belt-extension appears to be in combat with a similar figure (*Ill. 2–19*). The fanged gods may be twins; twins are prominent in South American mythology and may provide the answer to the puzzle of fanged god fighting fanged god. In any case, such scenes are rare.

A conflict takes place between the deity and a monster based on a marine lizard who has a snake tail; several scenes show the god cutting off this tail, which is possibly the source of his snake belt. Another less frequent encounter is with a round-bodied monster with spots on it. This creature has been called a "stone" monster, which is possible, but it is more likely a bivalve, since the only monsters the deity contests are sea creatures.

The deity was apparently wounded in one of the combats with a sea monster. Two anthropomorphic cormorants, one on either side, support him (*Ill. 2–8*). The cormorants, birds who plunge deep into the water, had perhaps brought him up from the bottom of the sea—indeed, if he is the sun, perhaps they had to rescue him every night. It appears to be the supreme god, not the fanged god, who is shown here: He always wears the sunrise headdress and stands straight-legged and awkward, like a rag doll. God the son always gives a sense of life and action, whereas this figure, like the sculptural figure on the mountain pots, is lifeless. Perhaps this stiffness of the figure rescued by cormorants is simply because he is unconscious. One could imagine a legend in which the supreme god, having once come down to the sea and been drowned, afterward sent his active son instead.

The active deity's faithful helper is an anthropomorphic lizard who wears a bird headdress (*Ill. 2–9*) and frequently stands by, ready to lend a hand, although it is clear that there are only certain occasions on which his assistance is needed (or only certain myths in which he plays a part). Another, although less frequent, servant of the deity is an owl, usually anthropomorphic. The owl, nocturnal like the deity's jaguar ancestor—if ancestor it is—would be an appropriate creature to accompany the fanged god on his journey through the night. The owl also appears independently and in various guises, and clearly had a more complicated role than the anthropomorphic lizard. Snakes, which are often depicted with the deity, especially the creator god, are represented not as companions or helpers but as symbolic devices or accessories. They usually appear in pairs, either flanking the god or appended to his headdress or belt.

2–7. A modeled and painted pot, with the fanged god emerging from a crab shell and holding a line with the fish monster on the other end. The monster has a human leg and arm and holds a knife.

2–8. The deity supported by two anthropomorphic cormorants who seem to be feeling his muscle and taking his pulse. They stand on a box with a step motif that may indicate a temple.

The deity is accompanied at times by a small, spotted animal—entirely animal and unanthropomorphized—who follows him like a pet and occasionally nips the crab monster. It is possible that this is a dog, as it has sometimes been called, yet the spots suggest a jaguar or a puma cub, although the markings are odd for a feline. Clearly the jaguar was the animal most closely associated with the deity, and, if it does not often accompany the deity, it is probably only because the deity himself was the essential jaguar (*Ill. 2–20*). The jaguar has had an influential mystique throughout pre-Columbian Latin America: The largest cat in the New World, it is a mysterious and powerful nocturnal predator, prowling at night along the waterways of the tropical rain forest. There are a number of naturalistic representations of felines in Mochica art giving evidence that feline cubs—preferably jaguars, although a puma might do if a jaguar could not be captured—were brought from beyond the sierras to the coast. Mochica artists knew exactly what they looked like (*Color Plate III*). Pots that show a man, presumably a priest, with a small cat at his side (*Ill. 2–10*), and other painted scenes that depict a feline tied outside a temple, give evidence that felines were kept by the priest for ritual or sacrificial use. The fact that several pots represent large cats with human prisoner figures suggests sacrifice, although the principal kinds of sacrifice scenes depicting the deity do not directly involve the jaguar.

The Mochica undoubtedly went into the mountains to make propitiatory offerings of human life to the creator god. One common sacrifice scene, depicted on modeled pots, takes place in the mountains, where, surrounded by peaks, a group of people, one of them holding a deer or other animal, stand around the sculptural form of the supreme deity. On top of the central mountain peak a figure is seen tumbling down, hair streaming downward; in the valley below, another figure lies dead or dying. The concept of two victims represents a theme of duality that is woven throughout the texture of Mochica art.

The other form of sacrificial scene represented on the modeled pots involves the fanged god and seems to take place in the sea (*Ills. 2–11 and 2–12*). One victim's body rides the crest of a breaking wave that merges into a step motif, surely a symbol of power, perhaps originally deriving from a stylization of mountains. The second victim lies on the lowest step. The fanged god watches from one side of the step-wave, and his lizard helper watches from the other. The step-wave scene may not actually be a scene of human sacrifice but one simply of death in the sea; victims of drowning may have been automatically dedicated to the fanged god. The combination of the wave with the step motif perhaps implies that the man who dies in the sea still belongs to the power of the mountains. The step-wave is one of the most widespread motifs in pre-Columbian art and must have had many levels of meaning.

The mountain sacrifice scene takes place only in front of the supreme god, the wave scene only in front of the fanged god. The

2-10. A seated man in elaborate dress with a jaguar cub.

2-9. The fanged god sitting opposite the lizard helper in bird headdress.

supreme god is indifferent to the fate of the victims, whereas the fanged god watches them. The victims of the two scenes are in identical positions. These scenes appear only on modeled pots. While the painted pots do not show the above ceremonies, they do depict a variety of scenes in which prisoners are about to be sacrificed, generally by beheading. In none of these scenes is the deity close by, as on the modeled pots.

There are curious omissions in the representation of godly activities. While the deity is shown in combat with monsters, he is never shown as a leader in human warfare, and pots with representations of him carrying conventional arms are extremely rare. While the godhead is frequently shown springing out of ears of maize or other vegetables, the deity is never shown actually planting (as he is shown hunting or fishing), and only infrequently is he shown holding a digging-stick. Although certainly the struggle for land and crops was of great importance to the Mochica, their religious—or, at least, mythological—emphasis was on activity in the sea rather than on the cultivated land. The coastal valleys were where the people were; the sea and the mountains were the realms of the deity. The sea was where mythic battle was done; the mountains were where ceremony was carried out.

2–11. A step-wave sacrifice scene, with the god watching from the side. One victim falls on the crest of the wave, the other victim lies on the lowermost step.

2–12. The same pot, with the lizard helper watching from the other side of the wave.

2-13. The radiant god holds a cup as the hawk creature approaches him. The body of the sky monster is represented by the bands of step motif and circles across the center of the pot. In the scene below, the god's litter rests with a jaguar in it. Weapons bundles are painted on the spout of the pot.

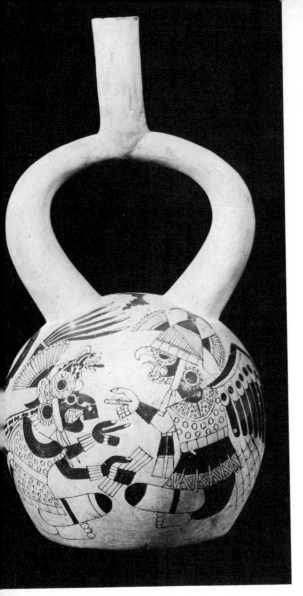

2–15. The moon monster, with a row of steps sprouting from his head, is surrounded by a painted design of an astral motif.

△
2–14. The fanged god, holding what appears to be a bundle of sticks, sits across from the hawk creature, who wears an elaborate warrior's helmet.

Scenes involving the deity probably have astronomical associations. Most early peoples were very aware of astronomical lore, and, certainly in Mesoamerica, astronomy and religion were closely linked. Too little is known of the Mochica to put forth any such theory with assurance, but it is quite likely that some of the scenes representing the deities actually depict astronomical events. The scene of the wounded god being helped by cormorants, for example, might represent the wounding of the sun in a partial eclipse.

38

2–16. The fanged god, in swirl-pattern shirt, attacks a naturalistic crab. The god has a knife raised in his right hand and grasps the crab claws with his left. His bent knees and coiled snake belt-extension give a sense of motion.

In late Mochica times, a new deity arrived on the scene, sharing importance with the fanged god. He wears a warrior's dress and helmet with knife, and has radiances that often end in snake heads projecting from his body. His armor seems to reflect an increasing spirit of Mochica militarism. He might well be called the "radiant god," and is the prototype of the later Chimú moon god, Sí. Like the fanged god, he also has feline dentition and is sometimes accompanied by a jaguar. He is always associated either with a litter or a raft.

39

2–17. A relief pot with the fanged god
subduing a crab-bodied monster. The
victor's grasping the conquered by the
hair was the common Mochica way of
showing defeat and suggests
decapitation. Both the deity and the
monster hold knives.

2–18. The fanged god "washing his
hair," apparently having just
emerged from the sea. At his feet
are two painted fish monsters with
knives, and, in the lower scene, two
rafts are anchored with stones.

2–19. A hammered gold plaque showing the fanged god facing his *alter ego*. They hold a rattlepole between them. Such poles apparently had rattles of shell or metal, with a head—perhaps a trophy head—at the top. The figure at the left has a conch shell over his left arm.

2–20. A pyramid with a ramp decorated with snail shells and prowling felines. In the shelter at the top is a figure with a Chavínoid mouth, undoubtedly representing the deity.

2-21. On this elaborate pot, the hawk creature holds a club and shield and rides a raft to which four small human beings cling.

He often appears in a raft on one side of a pot, with the fanged god in a raft on the other side. Usually the radiant god is shown in elaborate scenes (*Ill. 2–13*). A progression of scenes on different pots seems to show a sequence of his activities, in each of which uprooted plants play an important part. First, he is borne in a litter surrounded by various animals and monsters, a small jaguar riding with him. In another scene, he is shown arriving at a temple where he is greeted by an anthropomorphic hawk. In a third scene, the hawk creature is still there, and the fanged god has now appeared. On a lower level of the scene two sacrificial victims sit by the god's litter, in which a jaguar waits. It is tempting to think that this last scene might represent an astronomical event—with the radiant god as the moon, the fanged god the sun, and the hawk creature Venus—that is celebrated by human sacrifice. The plant association with the radiant god may well have had to do with the tying in of the agricultural calendar with the moon cycle.

2–22. A painted version of the deity as a crab, with the fish monster on a line. The crab shell is decorated with a characteristic Mochica fret and what are probably stylized jaguar markings. Pairs of snakes are painted on the spout.

The hawk creature, who accompanies the radiant god, is also dressed as a warrior and seems to have been a creature of considerable importance in his own right (*Ill. 2–21*). He occasionally rides alone in the radiant god's litter. One or two scenes show him seated beside the fanged god himself (*Ill. 2–14*).

In earlier Mochica pottery, before the advent of the radiant god, there is a fairly frequent representation, on both painted and modeled pots, of a "moon monster," a creature depicted on the painted pots as riding a crescent moon like a hammock, surrounded by astral motifs (*Ill. 2–15*). It is characterized by two rows of step motifs, one coming from the top of the head and one from the tail, each ending in a swirl, so that the step-wave motif is formed. The monster has a glaring eye, an open mouth, and prominently outspread claws, but it is hard to say what animal or animals it derives from. One pot indicates that it was a jaguar, but usually it is a dark, sleek, curving creature that rarely has feline dentition, but sometimes has a forked tongue. This creature, which usually appears alone, is also a Recuay motif. The fact that it is not frequent in later Mochica pottery probably indicates the growing importance of a moon cult worshiping the radiant god.

In later Mochica pottery there is frequent depiction of what is probably a sky monster, a two-headed creature that in certain scenes seems to indicate the demarcation between sky and earth (for instance, in the sacrifice scene involving the radiant god). In some cases, this monster arches over the fanged god, suggesting that he is in the realm of the sky. Both the fanged god's raft and the radiant god's litter are two-headed like the sky monster, indicating that the deities moved in a heavenly realm, perhaps carried by the sky monster.

It is difficult to interpret all the associations of the creatures represented in Mochica art. The Mochica must have believed in a god associated with wind, for instance, since wind would not only have been important to the fishermen but would also have been felt strongly as a presence in the coastal valleys. There must, too, have been a god associated with earthquakes, which were probably as frequent and severe then as now. This perhaps would have been the god of the mountains, the creator god himself, since he is associated with caves and probably with the heart of the earth as well as with the sky.

Chapter three

Messengers And Monsters

Mochica beliefs and style appear to have spread largely by conquest. In the Virú Valley, for example, Mochica influence was not a gradual one merged into the preceding Virú style, but one that took over all at once. The warlike nature of the Mochica is further indicated by the pottery—there are great numbers of painted battle scenes and of effigy warrior figures (*Ills. 3–1 and 3–2*)—as well as by the warriors represented in copper, silver, and gold.

Warriors wore shirts and kilts that sometimes seem to have been made of metal plaques or of reeds (*Color Plate IV*). They wore conical helmets, usually with a knife-shaped ornament at the top. They also had a knife tied to the belt; however, knives were never shown in use in a battle scene. Their weapon was a large club, and their defense a square or round shield or a sling. In battle, warriors surely also used spears ejected from spear-throwers, but the long-range fighting in which spears would be used is not shown on the pottery. The Mochica pot-painter was interested only in the hand-to-hand combat of the ultimate moment of battle when the decision would be made between victor and loser.

Warriors all have conventional movements, and many of them have common types of dress. In some cases, however, the garb of the defeated warrior—often curiously elaborated and improbable, as if to emphasize foreignness—seems to have been completely made up by the artist, who based the garments and gear on forms he knew, while devising new designs and motifs to make them as exotic as possible. At other times, it seems that Mochica warriors are fighting each other: They wear the same motifs on their clothing and carry the same sort of weapons. Perhaps these later scenes are meant to represent historical moments when the Mochica won the right to wear certain motifs. In any case, the painters do not seem to have been reporters who actually covered the story but artists who represented the battle scenes as history or legend, and according to rather static conventions —that is, showing the fighting in pairs, showing one man's head being broken with a club, another's helmet flying off, or yet another being grabbed by a lock of hair.

3–1. A pot with a painted frieze of warriors in battle. A warrior with a "swirl" helmet and shirt grasps the hair of one warrior with a square shield. Behind the winning warrior a helmet falls to the ground.

When the Mochica took prisoners, they stripped them, then tied their clothing and weapons to their clubs, and led them back, often with a rope around the neck, to be presented at a pyramid temple. A "weapons bundle"—a heraldic trophy consisting of a shield centred in the foreground, and, behind it, some combination of clubs, spears, spear-thrower, and often a sling—appears in scenes and as a motif by itself. The Mochica did not fight to kill (no one is ever shown dead in battle) but to take prisoners, who were probably used in sacrifices to their deity. Further scenes show the naked prisoners seated, apparently awaiting ceremonial decapitation. It was perhaps this moment that is symbolized by the warrior's knife, although it was not the ordinary warrior who committed the sacrifice, but rather monster helpers of the gods.

On another category of painted pots a man in warrior's dress with the head, wing, and tail of a hummingbird or a hawk marches or runs or dances, carrying a club and shield or a "weapons bundle" (*Ill. 3–3*). Is he a human being ceremonially dressed in the costume of a special order of warriors, or is this representation a metaphor for his character as a warrior? Is this a special creature—fantastic to us but perhaps very real to the Mochica—who was a mythical warrior-servant of the deity (for in at least two instances, one of these creatures has the deity's Chavinoid mouth), or does it represent the transformation of a human being into an animal? Such creatures appear in pairs on painted pottery or singly on modeled pots. They have the faces of hummingbirds, hawks, owls, foxes, deer, or even snakes. Whatever their significance, they probably do not represent castes of warriors, for such figures never appear in actual battle scenes. Scenes that show men striking each other or that show victorious warriors leading prisoners home always show straightforward human beings.

3–2. Kneeling on one knee, this modeled warrior holds a club and wears a nose ornament and a jaguar headdress with paws upraised like mountain peaks. The design on his garment probably represents small metal disks.

3–3. A double-fanged hawk with a human arm and leg holds a weapons bundle with a shield, club, four spears, and a sling. The most common way of anthropomorphizing birds or fish was to add this kind of leg and arm.

3–4. A lima bean with a human face and arm holds a weapons bundle.

Another category of partially human warriors carrying weapons bundles is that of the warrior with the body of a lima bean (*Ill. 3–4*). These bean-warriors sometimes also have the attributes of deer, jaguars, or foxes. Still other painted pots show human figures running through a landscape (*Ill. 3–5*), carrying bags that presumably contain lima beans (bags like those depicted in the hands of the runners have been reportedly found with beans in them). These figures are bare-chested and wear loincloths. Most commonly they wear a large metal plaque tied to an animal headdress with a chevron pattern (*Ill. 3–6*). In many cases, alternate runners have round and shovel-shaped plaques. Sometimes they wear a smaller variation of the deity's sunrise headdress. They run through sandy landscapes in which beans

3–5. A messenger with hands on the headdress ties sits cross-legged on a pot with a frieze of human-headed runners carrying bags across a sandy landscape. They wear nose ornaments and have painted faces. Hummingbirds plummet between the runners.

3–6. A headdress plaque of the type worn by messengers. The sheet gold has been hammered over a mold and cut, with holes at the feline head to allow attachment to a headdress. At either side is an upside-down bird like those often depicted in pottery scenes.

or cacti or pineapple plants are floating. Sometimes hummingbirds dart in among them. Like the pots representing warriors, those representing runners fall into two classes: those where the runners are human beings and those where the runners are anthropomorphic animals. A variety of animals—virtually all the animals in the Mochica repertory—are anthropomorphized in these scenes: the hummingbird (*Ill. 3–7*), the hawk, the puma, the jaguar, the deer, the fox (*Ill. 3–8*), the duck, the snake, the dragonfly, and the centipede. Sometimes there are fish runners dashing through waves.

Human-headed and animal-headed runners are never mixed in the same scenes, yet their movements and dress are alike. Do these scenes represent activities in the two different realms of the real and the supernatural? Are the human runners historical, as one presumes the warriors in battle scenes are? Do the animal-headed runners represent activity in a symbolic realm? In two of the animal-headed scenes, the destination is shown—a pyramid or temple decorated with the step motif—and, in one of these scenes, the deity sits on top of the temple, so that animal-headed runners seem to be messengers or servants of the deity. Perhaps the human-headed runners ceremonially re-enacted this mythical activity.

These runners or messengers make one think of the *chasquis*, the runners who traversed Inca roads to carry messages from one end of the Empire to the other. It is quite possible that the Mochica had, on a much smaller scale, roads and a similar system of runners. Since the Mochica runners carry bags of lima beans, and since various plants are pictured in the scenes with them (and the bag may well have contained other kinds of seeds as well as beans), the runners may possibly have gone in after the armies to take symbolic and practical seeds to be planted in new lands. Rafael Larco Hoyle has put forth a case for the use of lima beans as inscribed documents, and

3–7. A hummingbird runner carrying a bag. In front of him is the black-and-white tail of an anthropomorphic fox and a pineapple, or *Tillandsia*, with its roots showing.

3–8. An effigy fox-headed messenger sits cross-legged with hands on the ties of the headdress.

Victoria de la Jara considers them a means of recording numbers. Lima beans may well have been used in divination. Several scenes, in which lima beans are apparently being counted or interpreted by supernatural beings, indicate this. At the time of the Conquest, there was a game involving beans that may well have grown out of earlier ritual. There are Mochica scenes with two creatures sitting with beans and what appear to be bundles of sticks, which again suggests some sort of game of fate.

The depiction of fantastic creatures is not limited to warriors and messengers. As has been noted, the fanged deity battles monsters; he was rescued from the sea by anthropomorphic cormorants, and is most frequently accompanied by the anthropomorphic lizard helper. He is also sometimes assisted by an anthropomorphic owl.

Perhaps the most varied and mysterious role in Mochica mythology is that of the owl. Owls may be represented absolutely naturalistically; they also appear with a mixture of human attributes; still another category seems to represent a human being dressed as an owl, wearing an owl suit and an owl mask (*Ill. 3–9*). Owls of various kinds are depicted in scenes, and they also frequently appear alone as effigy pots, usually in some more or less human version. Owls frequently have double fangs; sometimes the owl has a stepped shirt like that of the deity, and in at least one case an owl appears seated on a throne. There are owl warriors but never owl messengers. The bird is often associated with ritual and sacrifice. Twice, wearing a white shift and carrying what looks like a sling, an anthropomorphic owl appears with the fanged god. One of these scenes is that of the runners coming to the temple where the god is enthroned; the other involves a game or ritual of "badminton." Sometimes an owl appears with a human head in one hand and a knife in the other; in another scene, an owl holds a knife to the throat of a man; in yet another, it appears in effigy with a large prisoner figure; and in still another, it has a human being on its wing. In this last scene, the man on the wing wears the step shirt of the fanged god and is possibly a sacrificial victim, dedicated to the deity, being carried to the other world by the owl.

The corpus of "demon" pots is very large. Almost all birds and animals appear in both natural and humanized forms and sometimes in more complexly compounded forms. But there are often differences in the contexts in which they appear and in the roles they seem to play.

Bats, usually anthropomorphized, appear with trophy heads and seem to be associated with sacrifice and ritual, although they are less frequently represented than owls (*Ill. 3–23*). They sometimes have the double fang. They do not appear as warriors or messengers. In addition to the specific hawk creature who participates in scenes with the fanged and radiant gods, hawks also appear frequently and usually anthropomorphically, as warriors, messengers, and as creatures carrying weapons bundles. Hummingbirds are also frequent both as warriors and messengers. In fact, a hummingbird is one of the most frequent runner types and usually the lead runner. Naturalistic hum-

3–9. The standing figure of a man wearing an owl mask and owl-wing cape. In his left hand he holds a small human trophy head.

3–10. A deer sitting and holding two young deer as a human mother would.

mingbirds appear in scenes with both runners and warriors. Hummingbird and hawk warriors often have the double fang. Anthropomorphic cormorants, as has been noted, were the rescuers of the deity. They also appear alone and as participants in painted sacrifice scenes, where they seem to be attending to the prisoners. Cormorants, unlike most other creatures, seem to have had benign and helpful dispositions. They are usually anthropomorphized, whereas other seabirds are usually represented naturalistically.

Deer are messengers and occasionally warriors. Deer with human arms sit as effigy figures (*Ill. 3–10*), and, in one scene, a naturalistic deer sits like a man *vis-à-vis* the fanged god. Deer also appear naturalistically in hunting scenes, with both human beings and the god as hunters. A deer is also shown in the arms of one of the participants in

54

mountain sacrifice scenes. Anthropomorphized foxes are rendered as separate effigy figures, and as both warriors and messengers. Occasionally, on painted pots, they appear realistically in a landscape. Seals are usually represented realistically, although they may sit or stand like men (*Ill. 3–21*). They appear in hunting scenes, but not as messengers or warriors. One group of effigy pots consists of birds, foxes, deer, or seals seated and playing a drum. Occasionally, a realistic rodent is shown nibbling on an ear of maize. Frogs and toads are not usually anthropomorphized but are combined with feline and plant features (*Ill. 3–11*), the plants undoubtedly denoting an association with water and, hence, with fertility. Other creatures depicted in both naturalistic and fantastic forms are snakes, dragonflies, and centipedes. Realistic lizards are sometimes rendered on painted or relief pottery, but the only instance in which the lizard is anthropomorphized is in the case of the lizard helper.

Curiously, although fish monsters are common in Mochica art, representations of realistically modeled fish are rare. Fish are shown occasionally in painted marsh or sea scenes, but rarely in other forms.

3–11. A frog with the clawed feet of a feline, swirls added at the ears and nose, two stalks of vegetables on the back, and a design of beans painted on the body.

However, one of the most common of all Mochica motifs is the ray. Representations of the ray run the gamut from realism through stylization to a combination of the essentials of the ray form with other Mochica motifs, particularly the stepped square. Octopi are sometimes pictured, as are shells. Realistic shells frequently appear, and there is also a shell monster.

The above list contains creatures native to the coast, but there are also frequent representations of animals from the sierras and the lowlands beyond. Llamas, highland creatures who may have carried loads to the coast, are frequently depicted, but always realistically and always on modeled pots. Monkeys, who were probably brought down to the coast from the lowland rain forest on the far side of the mountains, are usually anthropomorphized; in rare cases, they appear realistically. Jaguars, pumas, and possibly ocelots appear in both realistic and semihuman form. They appear as messengers but not as warriors.

3–12. A "fantasy" pot, with the wrinkled and distorted face of the fanged god with a snake earring. A seal head emerges from the top of his head. Water is indicated over the face at the right.

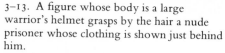

3-13. A figure whose body is a large warrior's helmet grasps by the hair a nude prisoner whose clothing is shown just behind him.

A number of animal or anthropomorphic creatures have the deity's double fangs. It is a question whether this denotes their own power or whether the fangs are a symbol of dedication to the deity, denoting that they are in the service of the god. Sometimes the deity's monster opponents also have double fangs that, in this case, must indicate demon power. Very often, animals will have some attribute of another creature—a jaguar will have the eye markings of a hawk, a deer will have the tail of a snake. Plants as well as animals sometimes bear not only the face of the deity but of a human being (*Ill. 3–22*).

In addition to the animal and plant pots, there are other groups of pottery whose meaning bewilders the modern mind. One of these is the "fantasy" pot that depicts an almost Picasso-like version of what is probably a water scene (*Ill. 3–12*). The distorted, wrinkled face of the deity appears among other elements—owls, seals, fish—in a modeled pot of uneven surfaces, which may represent the displacement of vision underwater. Since water is actually sketched on these pots, this would seem a reasonable reading, but their purpose remains mysterious. Several pots and a wall painting from the Huaca de la Luna show animated objects, particularly weapons and warriors' garments (*Ills. 3–13 and 3–14*); large helmets have small human legs, clubs have faces, and enormous kilts (*Ill. 3–15*) sprout tiny human features.

3-14. A stirrup-spout pot in the form of a helmet with round ear protectors.

3-15. A scene with the radiant god, at the right, shows various anthropomorphic animals and kilts with human heads and legs. At the bottom, an animated stake pulls a prisoner deer-man by a rope around the neck.

All of these fantastic pots raise questions of meaning or, at least, of the reasons for their production. One possible answer is that they represent a psychedelic experience on the part of the priest or shaman. One pot with animated objects shows a human figure in a little house who might well be a shaman "experiencing" such a vision. Present-day Indian shamans in the Amazon area use *Piptadenia* snuff and drinks made from *Banisteriopsis*, *Datura*, and other plants to achieve hallucinogenic religious experiences. A snuffing-tube was found in the Chicama Valley at the pre-ceramic site of Huaca Prieta. In one scene, the Mochica radiant god has an object that looks like a snuffing-tube, although it seems to be held more to the mouth than to the nose. But, while hallucinogens have had a long and prevalent history in South America, there is as yet no archaeological evidence for snuff-taking, or the use of other hallucinogens, in the Mochica period. A hallucinogenic cactus does grow, however, on the north coast.

Two stimulants were used by the Mochica, and their use is amply illustrated on the pottery (*Ill. 3–25*). One of these was coca. Coca leaves—from which cocaine is now extracted—were dried, cured, and chewed with a little slaked lime to draw the juice from the leaves. Coca is still chewed in the Andean highlands as a stimulant that promotes endurance, forgetfulness of hunger, and energy in a high altitude. In Mochica times, it was chewed by warriors before battle to give courage and endurance (*Ills. 3–16 and 3–18*). It also had ceremonial functions, and its use is indicated in scenes with the deity in the mountains (*Ill. 3–17*). The best coca is grown at a fairly high altitude, and so it may have been one of the things precious and holy to the Mochica because of its identification with the highlands as well as for its practical effects. W. Golden Mortimer reports that, at the turn of this century, Indians would throw coca into the air before beginning a trip into the highlands, to propitiate the mountain gods for the invasion of their domain. However, coca is a stimulant and not a hallucinogen. It is possible that, given potentiating circumstances—fasting or the consumption of other stimulants—it might be a factor in producing a hallucinated experience, but in itself it would not produce the kinds of visions shown in the pottery scenes.

The other stimulant used by the Mochica was chicha, a fermented corn beverage still common in the Andean region today. Chicha is also ritually associated on Mochica pottery and is primarily shown in scenes involving death and human sacrifice—at least, one assumes that it is chicha in the cups shown in these scenes, for chicha was associated with funerary ceremonies in the Andes. Again, chicha is not a hallucinogen and to those accustomed to hard liquors is barely intoxicating.

It is possible that in some of the less comprehensible representations the Mochica were showing, in a parable-like way, their myths and ceremonies. Perhaps they believed in the animation of weapons as modern man, in a less ingenuous way, "believes" in gremlins and the human spirit of planes, automobiles, and boats. There would have been an animism, or human or divine spirit, in animals or inanimate objects, probably related to belief in magic—a many-leveled magic that may well have changed meaning or emphasis through the centuries.

Moreover, the symbolic motifs that later probably came to have more secular meaning would have originally invoked a stronger kind of magic. These symbols, like the messengers and warriors, must have had both literal and figurative meanings. The step motif that appears on temples, on the litter of the radiant god, and on the cheeks of the dead probably originally denoted the mountains and the divinity thereof but later evolved into a symbol of secular status and power. The S motif is a symbol of water, but it also appears as a decoration on garments and must have had a more abstract meaning.

◁ 3–16. A warrior, kneeling on one knee and looking upward, has a lime pouch in his hand and is apparently taking coca before going into battle.

3–17. The deity in "prayer pose" is apparently involved in a coca-taking ceremony, with a bag of coca at his arm and a lime pouch in front of him. The two-headed sky monster arches over his head.

3–18. Another view of the same pot, showing one of three mortals taking coca. Behind him is what appears to be a weapons bundle. This ceremony may have been a blessing of weapons before a battle.

3–19. A man, probably suffering from leishmaniasis, holds a stirrup-spout vessel in one hand, a dipper or "corn-popper" in the other.

The swirl is probably also associated with water but became such a common motif that it must have assumed other meanings.

The swirl is often doubled, as is the Maltese cross motif. These doubled or reversed symbols relate to the Mochica obsession with dualism, one of the notable themes of the style. Twins have a special mythical significance in Indian America, and this theme of duality is prevalent in the Mochica world. There are two victims in most of the mountain sacrifice scenes, and two in the step-wave sacrifice. It is apparent that these are not before-and-after representations of the victim but that there were two victims. (One for the mountains and one for the sea? One for the sun and one for the moon? One for the agricultural earth and one for the irrigating water? One for fish and one for maize?) Pots have a painted scene on each of their two sides; sometimes the same scene is repeated, or sometimes a matching scene. Pots were sometimes—if not always—made in pairs. Objects that are depicted on the pots—Panpipes, plants, and pots—are often tied together in pairs; Panpipes are almost always shown tied together and played by a facing pair of pipers. Spouts may be painted half-dark and half-light, and the body of the pot may repeat this pattern in reverse so that a foursquare motif is presented (*Ill. 3–27*). A warrior's shirt and kilt are frequently half-dark and half-light, so that the whole costume

3–20. A man with an elaborate tattoo of a snake. His face does not show the general malformation of disease, and the nose and lip may have been deliberately mutilated.

produces four alternating squares. This compounding of duality into foursquare and checkerboard motifs was common.

Another common alternation of dark and light appears in face painting. The Mochica custom of face and body painting must have had its origins in the concept of magical protection from evil spirits, but it undoubtedly came to have other meanings, of both status and identification. Most of the late Mochica portrait heads have the face painted with a dark vertical rectangle at the outside; this was surely a status symbol. On earlier Mochica pots, face paint was more varied and may have been associated with certain rituals and activities, as well as being more closely related to magic. Circles, the Maltese cross, and doll-like eyebrows persisted as face painting into late Mochica times.

There is a kind of language in the decorative motifs and the face- and body-painting patterns. There was also a language of gesture, for gestures and postures were surely significant. The creator god sits like a statue and so differentiates himself from the fanged god whose knees are always bent as if he were about to spring. The prayer pose used by the deity himself in mountain ceremonies is perhaps an invocation to the creator god, although its meaning may be quite different from our associations with the pose—the lizard helper is

63

3–22. A potato with a human head that has the tuft of hair associated with prisoners. A profile head appears at the side, seeming to grow from one of the eyes of the potato.

3–21. A standing seal with double fangs.

also usually depicted in the prayer pose. In some of the mountain sacrifice scenes, each of the attendant figures makes a different gesture, but these gestures are repeated in different versions of the scene, so that it seems there was a particular learned gesture for each participant in the ceremony. Warriors kneel on one knee, possibly in obeisance to the god before going into battle. Modeled figures of messengers, either human- or animal-headed, sit cross-legged and have their hands under the chin on the tie of the headdress, a curious gesture that must have been significant. Each pose probably carried a special meaning.

64

I. A view from the top of the Huaca del Sol, looking toward the sea. Sand and scrub growth contrast with the cultivated fields that have irrigation. On top of the *huaca*, the rectangular adobes (typical of Mochica construction) form the bases of small rooms.

II. A gold rattle with the figure of a warrior with inlaid-turquoise eye and ear ornament. The rattle has a loop on top by which it can be suspended.

III. A small turquoise carving, 1½ inches high, representing an oversized feline behind a small man with a pack on his back. This motif of the feline as either protector or devourer of a human being appears in various Mochica representations. The eyes are inlaid.

IV. A pottery head of the fanged god with jaguar headdress, round, staring eyes, and half-painted face.

3-23. An anthropomorphic bat holds a jug and a cup that probably held chicha for ceremonial use.

3-24. An early portrait pot of a man with a double-bird headdress, unusual face paint, and doll-painted eyebrows. The ears probably had metal ornaments.

There was a general tendency in pre-Columbian cultures to think that a certain magic resided in diseased or deformed people, and the Mochica must also have believed this. Among the many types of creatures represented on Mochica pottery are diseased, deformed, or mutilated human beings (*Ill. 3–26*). A large number of Mochica pots are effigies of people suffering from leishmaniasis (*Ill. 3–19*) or leprosy. Both diseases cause deterioration of the skin at the nostrils and mouth, giving the appearance of a mummified face. The fact that people with these diseases resembled the dead might well have lent them a mystical prestige in the death-oriented culture of the Mochica. Cretinism, causing extremely short limbs or the absence of the intermediate parts of the limbs, is also commonly depicted. The blind are often represented, and people who were blind in one eye appear to have had a special magic. Some of the disfigured faces

3–25. A man with closed eyes, with a coca bag on his wrist and the headdress and ear ornaments associated with coca-taking. Figures with closed eyes appear frequently; this may indicate a state of trance rather than sleep.

3–26. A figure of a man with tattooed designs on his face. He appears to be suffering from a disease that causes jug ears and distortion of the face.

seem to have come by their physiognomies through age and battle scars. Sometimes there are footless or armless creatures; these paraplegics may have been veterans of the Mochica wars of conquest, or they may have given an arm or a leg for the god, as might be indicated in several of the painted scenes in which disembodied limbs are pictured.

Deformities have been interpreted by Rafael Larco Hoyle as the result of punishment by mutilation (*Ill. 3–20*), and this may at times be true, but the deformity of faces and bodies is almost always clearly due to disease rather than to deliberate mutilation. Moreover, the fact that these people had a magical significance and were not simply victims of castigation is indicated by their garments; some of them even wear attributes of the fanged god.

The range of Mochica representations is vast, yet not entirely free, for certain rules are followed. Distinct types of dress accompany certain figures, as do certain gestures. The occasions for realism and those for humanizing animals or combining forms were clearly separated. Some creatures are depicted in both realistic and fantastic forms, while others appear only realistically. One can draw reasonably neat diagrams of the transformations and associations, but this is only the first step in the re-creation of a complex structure of beliefs. The structure reflects a complicated history of development, with concepts appearing in different times and different places; it reflects, moreover, a social organization and way of daily life composed of many diverse elements drawn together to make up the substance of Mochica life.

3–27. A fish monster is painted on a light ground; the other half of the pot is dark. The stirrup spout is painted half-dark and half-light, reversing the tones of the body of the pot.

Chapter four

The Humboldt Current is one of the world's richest fishing grounds today, as it undoubtedly was in Mochica times. Fish would have been the important protein food, abundant enough to provide for all. Mochica fishermen must have gone to sea in something like the present-day *caballito*, the "little horse" of a boat, ten or eleven feet long, which is still in use at the Moche fishing village of Huanchaco (*Ill. 4–1*). The *caballito*, the same type of boat pictured on Mochica pottery, is made of four tapering cylindrical bundles of totora reeds tied together so that there is a pointed bow, a square stern, and a small, flat cockpit at the stern where the single occupant kneels or sits. John Gillin notes that, when he made his study thirty years ago, the entire population of Huanchaco, including children of ten, knew how to construct these craft. Today they are used for sport at the water's edge, but they are also sometimes employed by fishermen for line fishing, small-net fishing, and crab-catching at the shore.

Fishermen, in the larger wooden boats now commonly used for offshore fishing, normally go out sixteen to twenty miles, stay all night, telling time by the stars, and return at dawn. The Mochica must have gone as far offshore as the modern wooden fishing boats, a trip that would certainly have been hazardous and impractical in a raft the size of the *caballito*. The Mochica may well have made rafts larger than those that exist today. The rafts represented on the pottery often have a load of jugs on them—possibly containing chicha or water—indicating not only that the boat would have gone off for a time long enough to require the liquid, but also that the boat was large enough to carry the load of pots. Several other readings might be made of these scenes of the rafts with pots. Since it is generally a deity who is represented in the boat (*Ills. 4–2, 4–3, and 4–4*), these may have been ritual or mythical scenes, suggesting that the sun deity had enough liquid on board to last him for the journey through the night, or the moon god enough liquid to last him through the day. But even though these scenes are mythological, they must also have had a basis in reality and surely represent the equipment of men who did actually go to sea in fishing boats.

4–1. *Caballitos* drying beside a fishing boat on the beach at Huanchaco in the Moche Valley. Made of bundles of reeds tied together, they allow one person to sit in the concavity shown here at the bottom part of the raft.

4–2. The fanged god in a reed raft. In his right hand he holds a net with floats on it. He has apparently just removed a crab from the net.

It is also conceivable that boats could have been used for coastal trading, and that the pots pictured on rafts were trade pieces rather than sustenance for a voyage. The bulk of Mochica trade was probably between the coastal villages and the upper valley villages, and between the valleys and the highlands. Even so, the spread of conquest and objects indicates that there was traffic along the coast. It is quite likely that the Mochica had some sort of road system, later swallowed up by greater road-builders, the Chimú and the Inca. Land travel along the coast would have been faster than travel by sea, but if one had a large cargo, one might transport it more expeditiously on a raft. A boat could carry more than a man or a llama.

4–3. The radiant god in a raft, the ends of which are monster heads. A row of bottles is depicted below the deity. Running human legs at the bottom indicate that the raft is anthropomorphized.

4-4. Another view of the same pot, showing two round nets with handles projecting from the two animal-headed rafts. The fanged god rides in the raft to the left, with weapons bundles in front of him and an object like a harpoon in his hand.

4–5. A modeled seal sits on top of a painted scene showing a seal hunt. A man clubs one seal; the seal behind him is dripping blood; at the far right, another seal clings to a rock.

Fishermen today use nets that probably had Mochica prototypes. Something like the present casting net is depicted in painted fishing scenes. A circular net with a handle, pictured on Mochica pots, is probably a dip net. The modern two-man fishing net is similar to the net pictured in deer-hunting scenes on Mochica pots; such a net may have been used in the water as well as on land. If something like the present-day setline existed in the Mochica period, large rafts may not always have been necessary for catching big fish, for fish like corvina, bonita, and bacalao are caught with this net, which extends out into the water perpendicular to the shore. The pottery shows that Mochica fishermen also used a type of harpoon.

The sea provided edible seaweed, and the Mochica undoubtedly also caught crabs and salt-water shrimp along the shore, as fishermen do today; fresh-water shrimp were taken from the irrigation canals. William Duncan Strong and Clifford Evans, Jr., report finding almost no shellfish remains in the middens of the Virú Valley and conclude that, if the Mochica ate many shellfish, they ate them on the beach and left the shells there. The creatures are abundantly represented on the pottery, however.

4–6. A wooden figure of a prisoner with hands tied behind his back, found in the guano deposits on Macabí Island.

Trade on its simplest and most basic level must have existed between the fishing villages along the coast and the farmers who lived farther inland in the valleys. The coastal villages would have supplied not only fish but also guano from the offshore islands to be used as fertilizer. There are a number of these islands off the Mochica valleys, one important one—Macabí—off the Chicama Valley, and several off the Virú, Santa, and Nepeña valleys. These seabird droppings contain phosphates, nitrogen, and potash in such form and quantity that they are a splendid natural fertilizer. Guano has been an important fertilizer in recent centuries, and was also important in pre-Columbian times; the evidence for this is a number of objects found in deep layers of guano, some of them in clear Mochica style. Most of the Mochica artifacts appear to have come from Macabí Island (*Ill. 4–6*), and almost all of them are wooden figures representing nude prisoners with ropes around their necks. One might make a guess that these were offerings to propitiate the mounds (mountains?) of guano that formed on these islands. Some pots represent expeditions to, or ceremonies on, a guano island.

The farmers, taking guano and probably also fish for fertilizer from the coastal villages, would have produced the cotton for fishermen's nets, as well as maize, beans, and other vegetables and fruits for food. The major valleys inhabited by the Mochica reached the peak of their agricultural development in the Mochica period. Virtually no domesticated plants were added after this time. The list of food plants utilized by the Mochica is compiled largely from their representations on pottery (*Ills. 4–7 and 4–8*), although food remains have been found in burials, middens, and caches; for example, two hundred plant specimens were collected as part of the Virú Valley project. The list of domesticated food plants in the Mochica period compiled by Margaret Towle consists of maize, common beans, lima beans, peanuts, sweet potato, white potato, manioc, peppers, llacon, achira, crook squash, Hubbard squash, pepino, and gourds, which were possibly used for food as well as for utensils. Towle also lists fruits that may have been cultivated or given at least some horticultural care: chirimoya, guanabana, pacae, tumbo, granadilla, guava, lucuma, ciruela del fraile, papaya, avocado, and pineapple. Some cactus fruits were edible, and spines, of course, could be used as pins and combs. The algarroba tree, used for shade and structural material, also produced a nourishing bean used for both food and medicine. Even today, the algarroba is an important resource, for it grows in virtual desert and has an extraordinary variety of uses. It is still used for house construction and for folk medicine, and it has newer uses as fencing and animal fodder.

Maize is still the most important crop grown for home consumption in these valleys. Its importance to the Mochica is obvious from its pottery representations, the most numerous of which show the head of the fanged deity emerging from the ears of maize. Moreover, maize has also been found in burial offerings. It was eaten as a vegetable, and prepared either by boiling or roasting. The stems were

4–7. A pot in the form of a squash.

4–8. A pot depicting a bowl full of peanuts.

4–9. Lima-bean warriors battle on the body of this pot. More realistic beans decorate the spout, but even these, like the warriors, have a half-dark, half-spotted pattern.

pressed for a sweet juice, and the kernels used as an oil source. It was important also as the basis of chicha—made from a mash of crushed kernels, chewed by women—which was a ceremonial drink strongly associated with scenes involving death and the dead.

Lima beans have a distinct position in the category of vegetable representations on Mochica pottery (*Ill. 4–9*). They are the only vegetable that appears truly anthropomorphized. With heads, arms, and legs, lima beans are shown as warriors and messengers, in both painted and modeled versions. There are naturalistic beans on painted pots, but they do not appear at all in their naturalistic form in modeled pottery. In the landscape of various scenes, lima beans float in the air, often with other plants or fruit, and they appear in the air in various ritual scenes. It is possible that, although the common bean was a staple, lima beans were not eaten, being used for ritual purposes only.

In addition to the food plants, various other plants—for example, cotton—were raised or, at least, utilized. One of the most important of these was *caña brava*, a large grass growing in swamps that was used for house construction, baskets, utensils, and so on. Other plants were used for dyes and medicinal purposes. Gourds were important as utensils. (In the more modest homes in these valleys today, one is still served chicha in a gourd cup, which may be decorated with an ancient Mochica design.) The Mochica farmer's principal tools were the hoe and the digging-stick, usually made of algarroba wood, sometimes with a copper point. Gillin also mentions narrow-bladed copper spades as Mochica tools.

Mochica farmers had irrigation canals, although they were not the inventors of canals in this area. Irrigation on the coast may have begun as early as the Coastal Chavín period and probably grew out of the use of flood-water irrigation. It surely existed in Gallinazo times and was expanded by the Mochica and then by later people. Some of the Mochica canals are still in use (*Ill. 4–10*). Water control would have developed along with a population increase, the need for more food for more people, and the greater social organization that larger villages and communication between them implies. The problems of water were complex. Sometimes the rivers on the north coast are dry or have little water for long periods of the year. Water is most abundant in March and scarcest in October. In the rainy season, there may be floods and much water goes unused into the sea. It is doubtful that the Mochica built dams to cope with this problem. The rivers that come from the Cordillera Negra, on the western side of the Continental Divide, have less water than those that originate in the Continental Divide itself. However, the amount of water does not necessarily correlate with the efficacy of the irrigation system, since the small Nepeña, for example, which comes from the Cordillera Negra, irrigates nearly as much land as the large and long Santa, because all the Nepeña water is utilized.

The Mochica irrigation canals are impressive and ambitious works. They were often carefully planned constructions, built along the edge of hills and across *quebradas*, on embankments of earth and adobe.

V. A gold mask with inlaid-shell eyes, from the Huaca de la Luna, Moche Valley, probably representing a chieftain.

VI. The Huaca de la Luna, with the Cerro
Blanco behind it, seen from the Huaca del Sol.
The foreground area, covered with scrub growth,
was once a habitation site.

VII. The top of an inlaid ceremonial digging-
stick, from the Tomb of the Warrior-Priest at
the Huaca de la Cruz in the Virú Valley. The
fanged god stands above a very small figure.
This idea is paralleled in the burial itself, for the
body of a young boy was found in the tomb
with the Warrior-Priest.

They not only channeled water within each valley, but the irrigation systems of the Chicama and Moche valleys, for example, were connected. The canals sometimes had defensive walls, because the coastal peoples were very vulnerable: If the canals were destroyed by enemies, it was a sure way of cutting off a large part of the food supply. Even today there is a strict control of the use of irrigation water. In the past, the use of this water must have been an important part not only of the political administration but of the ceremonial life as well. In the Virú and Mochica valleys, within living memory, there have been festivals in connection with the cleaning of the ditches before the waters come down from the mountains in full force in December.

There is evidence that the pre-Conquest irrigation system was considerably larger than that which exists today. There are various possible reasons for this. Certainly this shrinkage of the water system probably began at the time of the Conquest, when there was a considerable population decrease. It is also possible that there may have been a climatic change. But the most likely reason for the present state of the canal system is that two of the three present major commercially grown crops of the north coast—rice and sugar-cane—use more water than the major pre-Columbian crops (maize, for instance, requires little water), and, therefore, the water, more intensively used, is not available for such a large area as in the old system. Cotton, the third modern commercial crop, was also grown in pre-Columbian times and requires little water.

Irrigation caused the Mochica farmer problems as well as benefits. One of his chores is indicated by hillocks, investigated in the course of the Virú Valley project, which apparently consist of saltpeter. The irrigation of the soil would have leached the mineral salts from the earth, causing them to form a hard crust. Early farmers apparently had to remove this crust, and then piled it up on one side of the field. The modern plow, of course, obviates this problem.

One of the interesting Mochica iconographic problems is the frequent representation of plants in the scenes on the painted pots. Cacti and *Bromeliaceae* appear with their roots showing, floating in the air, especially in battle scenes and scenes with messengers. The fact that the roots are showing would indicate that they are not there simply as part of the landscape. One might make a number of guesses about their presence in this uprooted form. The appearance of plants in the scenes with messengers and beans suggests that these scenes involve some sort of divination about crops. Their appearance in the battle scenes might indicate the importance of gaining new land in which to plant crops. Their appearance in other scenes, including sacrifice scenes, might show that they were some sort of offering. In several scenes depicting a ceremony involving the radiant god, one attendant figure is shown holding an uprooted algarroba tree. There must have been some ritual or rituals that involved the uprooting of plants. Whatever their meaning on the painted pots, the plants surely had a significance highly charged by the needs of an agricultural people who had to struggle for land to cultivate.

4–10. A Mochica canal in the Moche Valley.

Protein sources on the land were poor: Beans provided vegetable protein, but animals were scarce. Deer were certainly hunted, but they were not abundant, and were at best the food of the upper class. Deer-hunts depicted on pottery show that deer were driven into nets by runners with clubs, where they were then speared by richly dressed men (*Ill. 4–11*). It is possible that there was a ritual aspect to these deer-hunts, and the deer meat may have been eaten only by the chieftains on ceremonial occasions. In addition to the spears used for deer, the Mochica seem to have used a blowgun to shoot birds (*Ills. 4–13 and 4–15*), and clubs to attack seals (*Ill. 4–5*), which they must have used for both food and skins. Lizards (*Ill. 4–17*) may have been trapped for food, as they sometimes are today, when a long roll of matting is stood like a fence across a field and the lizards are driven toward it. Not intelligent enough to get away, they are trapped there. John Gillin describes expeditions to the nearby mountains in the moist winter season to gather the large ground snails that appear at that time. These are steamed and eaten. Such snail-hunting expeditions are pictured on Mochica pottery (*Ill. 4–12*).

As in the rest of pre-Columbian America, there were no draft animals. Llamas were certainly brought down from the highlands, and, judging from the pottery representations (*Ills. 4–14 and 4–16*), they were used as pack animals, but a llama can only carry about a

4-11. An elaborate representation of a deer hunt. The richly dressed man—perhaps the deity himself or an impersonator of the deity—is clubbing a deer. The painted scene below shows a speared deer as well as the net into which the deer have been driven.

4–12. A cruet-shaped pot showing land snails like those that are hunted today in the hills; these, however, have monster heads.

hundred pounds and could not have been used for heavy transport. Since llamas are indigenous to high altitudes, it is also questionable how well they would have endured on the coast if they were used as work animals. They may have been used only on trips to and from the coast, and perhaps, since it had a special meaning from its association with the mountains, the llama may have been used only to transport ritually significant material. The appearance of sacrificed llamas in burials reinforces this theory. It is also possible that they were eaten, but they cannot have been plentiful enough to have been a major food source.

The mountains would have produced the copper, silver, and gold used to make ornaments and tools for the coastal valleys. Although wool is not common in Mochica textiles, it was used to some extent; the finest wool would have come from the vicuñas and alpacas of the highlands. In return for these goods, the lowlanders would have provided dried or salted fish and certain plant products that could not be grown in the cold altitudes of the highlands.

Probably the most important fact about Mochica livelihood was its organization. The Mochica had to be well organized in order to survive in the unfriendly climate of coastal desert and steep, barren mountains. Water usage had to be controlled and developed by an organized society, trade had to be regulated to keep up the flow of goods over wide and diverse areas, and armies had to be assembled to protect water and trade, and to fight for new lands that had then to be brought into the scheme of organized Mochica life.

The attempt to reconstruct Mochica social structure from the pottery representations is limited by the fact that the people on the pots generally have ritual or religious associations and therefore do not tell as much as they might about the total social picture. What is indicated—not only by the pottery but by architecture and other crafts—is much like what is known or guessed about other pre-Columbian societies. There was certainly an upper class, which undoubtedly combined sacred and secular power. The secular rulers may have been the chief priests (*Ill. 4–18*). In any case, the priests also had a great deal of power, and must have directed rituals that were thought to have guided the fate of agriculture, water supply, fishing voyages, trading journeys, warfare, and astronomy. Indeed, one feels, in looking at Mochica pottery, that another form of their obsessive dualism was that everything they did was half-religious and half-practical. As time went on, there may have been an increasing secularization—the great quantity of portrait heads seems to indicate this, for these heads do not relate directly to deities or demons, or to the sustenance of daily life; although they may have had magic power, they are still monuments to individuals (*Color Plate V*). Militarism undoubtedly also increased with time, indicated, for example, by the advent of the radiant god. Certainly warriors were an important class at all times, next in prestige to the chieftains and priests. The Mochica civilization must have been dependent, not only on the aggression of the army, but on its defense.

4-13. An unusual pot showing a man shooting at a bird with an oversized blowgun. The foliage of the tree in which the bird sits is painted on the bowl of the pot.

Aside from the mysterious representations of messengers and mutilated persons, we do not know a great deal about other classes of people, except for musicians, who are shown as richly dressed and seem to have special status; they may, in fact, have been priests. The people who were most directly responsible for our impression of the Mochica were the artisans, and about them we know nothing except for the testimony of their skill. Pots do not represent pot-makers, nor do they show goldsmiths or woodcarvers, architects or mural painters. Artisans were essential to the whole Mochica culture, but it is difficult to know what social status they may have had.

4-14. There are occasional representations of a man on the back of a llama. However, a llama cannot carry a man very far, especially when it is also burdened with saddlebags. The meaning of these pots remains mysterious.

4-15. A spotted bird with a young bird at its side. representations of animals and birds with their young are fairly common in Mochica art.

4–16. A kneeling llama with a pack on its back and a rope through its ear. Llamas were guided by this rope. This llama has elaborate painting on its forehead, eyes, and mouth.

4–17. An early Mochica pot with a lizard painted on it.

4-18. A portrait of a man with "log" earrings, typical face paint, and a headdress in which the wave motif has been transformed into a series of bird heads.

5–1. The Huaca del Sol, seen from the Huaca de la Luna, about 546 yards away. Now badly eroded, the Huaca del Sol—the largest adobe structure in the New World—seems to repeat the shape of the mountain in the background. In Mochica times, the foreground area contained habitation sites.

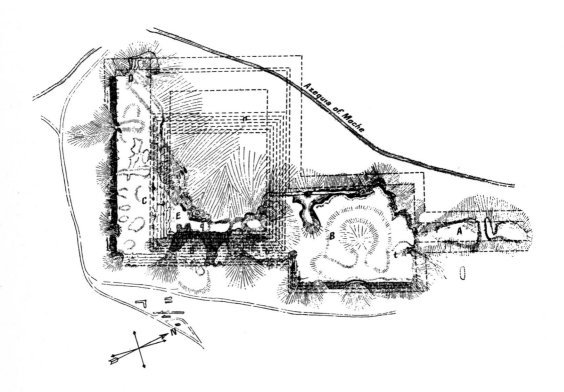

5–2. A plan of the Huaca del Sol. *A* is a causeway leading to the platform at *B*. The pyramid is marked *E*. There is another platform at *C*. The length of the structure from *B* through *C* is about 250 yards. Platform *C* goes back about 149 yards.

Chapter five

Architects And Artisans

The Mochica constructed their own "mountains" in the coastal valleys. Massive constructions of solidly piled adobes typify Mochica ceremonial architecture. The labor required to build them is another evidence of Mochica social organization—the thought of producing this number of adobe bricks is staggering. Gillin describes the manufacture of adobes in the village of Moche in the 1940's: This is probably much the same technique that was used in ancient times. Adobes were made by specialists of a clayey dirt, dug loose in the ground and then puddled with water. The dirt was mixed with grass cut one or two inches long. It was then carried in sacks to flat ground, where it was pressed into a wooden frame. When it had been smoothed with a spade, the frame was removed, and the adobe was slid off onto clean, flat ground and left to dry in the sun for about a week. In the Mochica era, large pyramids were built by constructing walls of these adobes side by side, so that the mass was actually built sectionally. The Huaca del Sol, the largest solid adobe structure in the New World, was apparently built all at one time in this manner. The Moche River has flooded and cut into the pyramid, revealing its inner construction. It is possible that there is a smaller, earlier core inside, but this is not apparent.

Many Mochica ceremonial structures are built on top of, or are attached to, earlier buildings. As is the case in other pre-Columbian areas, Peruvian builders did not always start afresh, and older buildings were sometimes used as the core for newer ones. Gallinazo structures lie at the heart of some Mochica buildings, and some Mochica buildings were later elaborated by Tiahuanaco-Huari additions. The pyramid-mounds continue a Gallinazo tradition. There are no great fundamental differences between Gallinazo and Mochica architecture, but Gallinazo structures are generally smaller and built of cane-marked adobes. Although adobe manufacturing techniques change from period to period, they also overlap. In the Virú Valley, all cane-marked adobes were found in Gallinazo structures and plain-surfaced adobes in Mochica remains. Farther north, early Mochica constructions were also, at least sometimes, made of cane-marked adobes. The Mochica also knew of *tapia*, a material

5–3. The Huaca del Brujo on the shore of the Chicama Valley. The cuts were apparently made fairly recently to obtain adobes.

consisting of larger molded blocks of sun-dried clay, but its use was infrequent. Occasionally, buildings had foundations of unworked stone. Poles and beams of wood from the algarroba tree were used to support or bind the construction.

Gordon R. Willey puts official or major Mochica buildings into three principal classes: pyramids, palaces, and fortifications. The pyramids were generally quite steep and often had room structures on top. Some were built in open valley country, and some on hills, either on the top or on the lower slope. While some pyramids were isolated, pyramids and palaces were often associated. The Huaca del Sol (*Ills. 5–1 and 5–2*) faces, across a space of some five hundred meters, the Huaca de la Luna, a construction of the palace type, with rooms surmounting a platform (*Color Plate VI*). In the Virú Valley, the Huancaco pyramid is incorporated within the palace group. The palace-type buildings seem to have been public buildings for religious and/or governmental use. An example of the third type of construction in Willey's classification—the fortification—is Facalá. This structure holds a strategic position, placed on top of a hill, with good observation over the valley, and in a position near a canal that it might presumably defend; it is also close to the hills that line part of the valley on one side. Hilltop fortifications go back to Salinar and Gallinazo times. The pyramids, of course, may also have functioned as fortifications.

96

5–4. A detail of an inner wall of the Huaca del Brujo shows the use of adobes to form decorative geometric patterns. In the lower left corner, it can be seen that some of the adobes are cane-marked.

Often Mochica buildings had some relationship to a hill, either on top of it, as with Facalá (which appears also to have had a Gallinazo construction), or in front of it, as with the Huaca de la Luna. Burials were also often made at the base of a hill, as at Cerro Vicús. In many cultures of the world, high places are sacred, and surely the Mochica hills must have had a special mystique as miniature local mountains. Even today in the Moche Valley, one is told of legends of the Cerro Blanco on which the Huaca de la Luna leans.

There is one circular mound with a ramp, reported by Willey in the Virú Valley. Circular platforms often appear in pottery representations, but their frequency probably relates more to the nature of the pottery medium than to the number of actual architectural constructions of round form.

The outer walls of buildings were coated with clay plaster and whitewash, and painted either in solid colors or designs or, as at Licapa or the Huaca del Brujo (*Ills. 5–3 and 5–4*), with a low-relief, textile-like pattern of adobes, which was also painted. Traces of figurative paintings have been found on walls lining courtyards and at various places within buildings. In 1910 Eduard Seler found a painting of two figures, one of which was an animated warclub, within the Huaca de la Luna. This disappeared, but in 1925 a similar painting was found in the same structure. One of the richest finds of wall paintings was in buildings at Pañamarca in the Nepeña Valley. Here three large panels were found in a room, as well as a procession of warriors painted along a wall. Generally, however, painted wall decoration is badly preserved. The wall paintings are similar in style to the paintings on pottery, but the color range is not so limited. A. L. Kroeber notes as many as seven colors (black, white, red, gray, yellow, brown, and blue) on one example of wall painting. The outlines of the subject matter were incised in plaster, then painted in black, and the colors were then painted within the outlined spaces.

Plazas and walled enclosures also appear in Mochica architecture. Willey points out the existence of large, empty, walled enclosures, reflecting the warlike nature of the times, as one of the outstanding differences between Gallinazo and Mochica sites in the Virú Valley. There are also defensive walls, dating from the Mochica period in the Virú Valley, which fortify a *quebrada*, mark off a defensive territory, or protect a watercourse. Such walls in the Upper Moche Valley may also have dated from this period, although their present structure dates from a later time. Walls were made of large boulders or adobes used in a sectional construction like that of the pyramids.

As for ordinary dwellings, the houses commonly seen in the coastal valleys today probably continue the style of ancient prototypes. House construction is still simple, since, in this climate, a house needs to be neither insulated nor well roofed. Two types of houses are represented on pottery. Modeled pots appear to represent houses made of adobe and placed on a platform or pyramid (*Ill. 5–5*). These houses seem to have been either religious structures or the houses of important individuals. Such houses sometimes have in front of them

5-5. This pot represents two houses on a striped base that forms two steps. The upper house has the step-triangle and angular-swirl motifs. The lower house has three war clubs protruding from the roofpole, and a striped roof.

5–6. A pot showing a house on a round, tiered platform with alternating rows of painted knives and step-triangles. The roof has a Maltese cross and a double-stepped roofcomb. Such decoration may actually have existed on buildings.

5–7. A scene in front of a house with a double-stepped roofcomb. The figure at the right has a pack on his back and hands clasped in the "prayer pose." The figure facing the door seems to be wearing widow's garments.

what appear to be mourners or worshipers (*Ill. 5–7*), and sometimes they have an oversized snake slithering through them or looking out the door. They have gabled roofs, which may or may not have had, in reality, the stepped roofcomb shown on the pottery (*Ill. 5–6*). Such a roofcomb would be possible to construct with adobes, but the fact that adobe houses today are not strongly roofed suggests that a similar construction in Mochica times would not have borne the weight of such a decoration. The decoration may have been merely a symbol used on the pottery to indicate that this was the house of an important person, or a house with power or prestige. The "knife" that often appears between the two sides of the roofcomb of these houses must certainly have been only a pottery symbol. The frogs or felines that appear on some pottery house roofs further suggest that the pottery often represents symbolic, not actual, ornaments. As usual in Mochica art, one has to try to make distinctions between what is a representation of objective reality and what is a spiritual or abstract concept.

Whereas modeled pots usually depict solid houses that seem to have been made of adobe, painted pots represent the type of modest house commonly seen along the road today in the northern coastal countryside. Houses on the painted pots are shown as open-walled, with a roof and rude posts at the corners. Their openness was quite likely an artistic convention to enable the viewer to see the person or scene usually shown inside the structure. The real houses probably had cane siding as the modern houses do. Modern houses also have algarroba posts at the corners, and a slanting roof that may have either a single or double pitch. Roofs of present-day houses consist of a thin thatch of cane or reeds, intended not to keep out rain but to give shade and privacy. The *quincha* type of wall utilizes upright canes inserted side by side in the ground. The upright canes are then interlaced with horizontal canes, usually one series in the center height of the wall, and another near the top. The canes are usually plastered with moist mud. Totora shelters, usually temporary structures today, are made of mats of woven reeds attached to a framework of saplings. Whereas the cane structures are made of *caña brava*, the totora shelters are made of the same cattail from which rafts are made.

Foundations of ancient houses may have been of stone or adobe, but floors were surely of hard-packed earth, as they still frequently are. Pottery figures are sometimes depicted holding a roll or lying on a partially rolled-out mat. At the time of Gillin's report, and to some extent today, poorer people still sleep on such mats placed on the earth floor. The more primitive fireplaces consist of three or four stones placed on the ground to support a cooking vessel. This is surely an ancient method.

Mochica-period dwellings in the Virú Valley, according to Willey, were commonly within rectangular enclosed compounds or in agglutinated villages, where the houses were attached. These "villages" might have only a few rooms or as many as seventy or so.

The architectural art was impressive for its scale and certainly at times for its decoration, although we have few opportunities to

5–8. A bowl with a wide, flanged lip, with scenes from a weaving shop. Weavers with backstrap looms work in house structures with rooftrees and bundles of reeds forming the roof.

judge the latter, since little of the decoration survives. Other crafts, however, enable us to appreciate Mochica artistic and craftsmanly skill, although some of these have also suffered fatal ravages of time. Textiles, for instance, have had a hard job of survival. Textile remains are infrequent and in poor condition because of the amount of saltpeter in the sands of the north coast. Max Uhle, for example, found no textiles at all in his excavations of more than thirty tombs at Moche. Most textiles that have been found in burials disintegrate as soon as they are exposed or touched, so that there is little left to judge from.

5–9. The realism of the face of this blind old man contrasts with the simplicity of the globular body. He wears a headdress like those being made in the weaving shop, and a sort of badge on a plain, long-sleeved tunic.

5–10. A man holding up a shirt with a step-triangle and angular-swirl border. The shirt was likely an offering.

However, the fragments that do survive show that textile craftsmanship was apparently advanced and of considerable skill.

Weavers were surely women. Female burials in the Virú Valley have disclosed weaving equipment placed with the bodies of women who were presumably weavers in life. A bowl in the British Museum shows a series of scenes in a workshop, with women sitting at back-strap looms that are supported by algarroba posts (*Ill. 5–8*). (These posts hold up the roof of the house, so that one can see plainly the building construction. Some of the posts are straight and look like modern finished wood; others retain the gnarled shape of the tree.) There is evidence that this is not a commonplace commercial workshop, and the number of pots floating in the spaces above the weavers is a clue to the significance of the scene. The pottery is not everyday ware but ceremonial or mortuary ware. It is quite likely that this was a shop, perhaps under religious jurisdiction, that specialized in the manufacture of cloth for burial. It may even represent preparations for a specific burial, that of someone of importance. One of the vases has a rope tied around the neck, a characteristic of pots that appear in funerary scenes, and next to it is a pot with sprigs tied at the neck, also seen in funerary scenes. Unfortunately, some of the surface is damaged, so that it is difficult to see what is perhaps the most significant scene, that in which a large figure in a striped shirt is seated on a throne, facing a seated figure who seems to be giving him offerings. The other variant scene (in which there are the two pots with sprigs at their necks) shows another seated figure handing, or being handed, a bowl. There are four figures in this scene, all of whom have the sort of headdress common on the portrait jars, and three of whom have dark faces, presumably painted.

Some of the women are shown making material used for the kind of headdress most frequently seen on portrait vases—what was apparently a white cloth, usually with a design on it, and a sort of rick-rack braid on the edge (*Ill. 5–9*). This angular edging relates to the step motif and was surely a sign of status. In some of these scenes in the workshop, this cloth is shown on the loom, but a piece of it is also shown floating in the space above the loom. The headdress itself was a longish band wrapped around the head in a conventionalized manner, and here we see the strips of it in the process of manufacture. The cloth being woven has typical Mochica motifs. One headdress has a stylized ray or skate, and there are two shirts (or possibly separate pieces of the same shirt) with a ray design. One weaver is constructing a shirt with a step design. At least one weaver is working on a ray-pattern cloth, and yet another is making a headband with the angular S.

Some textile specimens were reported by the Columbia University unit from excavations in the Virú Valley. Cotton was the most important staple in these fabrics; only one of the Mochica specimens contained wool. Most of the cotton yarns were of single ply, and the maximum loom width was sixty centimeters. Plain weaves and twill weaves and also gauze construction were reported, as well as tapestry and one example of double cloth.

5–11. A gold earspool, about 3 inches in diameter, depicting a man holding a spear thrower. This man represents the radiant god. Turquoise is set into the circular elements that project from his headdress.

Although textiles are scarce, we know a great deal about clothing, if not from cloth then from the pottery representations of garments. Depending on status or occupation, men wore trunks or a sort of kilt or a tunic or long shirt. With the trunks or kilt, they sometimes wore a shirt, often with sleeves, although certain figures are represented as bare-chested. Some figures wear a mantle or cloak. Judging from the existing textile fragments and from the workshop pot, the designs on these garments were woven, not painted. Although the designs on examples of Mochica textiles are closely related to those found on Mochica pottery, the existing fragments show more elaborate designs than are shown on the pottery; simplification would have been necessary for the pot-painter's art. The trunks are usually represented as either solid-colored or striped. The kilt is usually plain or half dark and half light, although some have an elaborate lower edge. There are plain, long, light-colored tunics with sleeves that may have designs at the cuffs and a sort of badge at the neck. This badge might be either woven or painted on the cloth, or it may represent a separate decoration of another material.

Mochica shirts have varied designs. Most frequent is the stepped design worn by the fanged god. Warriors often have a shirt that is half dark and half light (in vertical divisions) and a kilt of the same pattern in reverse, so that the whole costume makes a foursquare checkerboard pattern. They sometimes wear shirts with the swirl motif or the Maltese cross or a polka-dot design. The shirts held up by effigy figures have a greater variety of patterns than is seen on those that are worn by figures (*Ill. 5–10*).

Cuffs and kilt borders sometimes have decorations in the form of common Mochica motifs—the angular S, the stepped square, and the like. Some figures wear garments with a wide bertha at the neck, which may be decorated, often with a pair of snakes. The bertha is frequently a part of the costume of the fanged god and may represent a broad necklace rather than a cloth garment.

Headdresses are of a wide variety. In addition to the typical head-dress found on portrait vases, there are the warriors' helmets, pro-bably of bronze; the runners' headdresses, which had plaques of gold or copper; the animal headdresses, which apparently had copper heads and feet attached to cloth; the bird headdresses made of feathers. There is another type of headdress, frequently associated with coca-takers, which seems to represent *ullucho* fruit, whether the real fruit or some imitation. There are some rather odd headdresses in the form of toques or pillboxes or beanies. The headdress of the fanged god frequently had a feather fan at the back. Feather shirts and ear orna-ments and other accessories existed in other parts of the Peruvian coast and may well have been used by the Mochica.

Some warriors appear to wear a sort of reed armor, and other ele-ments of clothing show what are probably nontextile decoration: belts have a row of shells or metal bells; shirts seem to have small disks of metal sewn on them; and various shirts, belts, kilts, borders, and helmets appear to be made of small plaques of metal, probably sewn to a cloth base.

Although there were other fine metallurgists in Peru at this time, the Mochica were particularly advanced. The Chavín people had been working hammered and cut gold for centuries before the Mochica. The Mochica continued these processes and developed other metallurgical techniques. The important process of lost-wax casting was first developed by the Mochica. In the far north, fine braiding and granulation were used. The Mochica worked not only gold but silver and copper, and Rafael Larco Hoyle reports that lead has been found in Mochica graves. Copper was used in sheet form, and was also cast for tools and ornaments (*Ills. 5–12 and 5–31*). Mochica artisans could solder and weld and use gold washes. Gold was also used as a setting for other materials; for instance, gold earspools

5-12. A copper mask with eyes inlaid with shell and pyrite; about 8 inches high.

(Ill. 5–11) were inlaid with turquoise and shell. Headdresses, helmets, ear and nose ornaments, bracelets, and beads were made of metal, as were clubheads and tips for digging-sticks. Gold *repoussé* headdresses often had cutout designs or danglers attached with gold wires. There was also small sculpture in the round made from hammered gold; the pieces were probably hammered over a stone matrix and then joined with solder. Another use of metal was as adornment for the pottery: Gold nose rings and copper bracelets are sometimes found on effigy figures.

Although large stone sculpture was nonexistent in the Mochica *œuvre*, small objects were carved from various stones *(Ill. 5–13)*, including turquoise or chrysocolla, or shell and bone *(Ill. 5–14)*, and were often inlaid. There are also numerous objects—decorative, functional, and symbolic—that were carved from wood. Gourds, too, were incised and inlaid.

5–13. A stone bead in the form of a prisoner's head (possibly decapitated). The ears have been drilled as if for ear ornaments, and the eyes were possibly inlaid. One inch high.

5–14. A bone spatula handle in the form of a clenched fist and a forearm incised with scenes of large bird-headed warriors and small human figures.

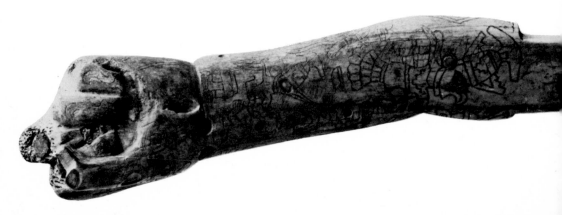

5-15. A wide-spouted effigy pot of an anthropomorphic seal with a drum.

5–16. A scene showing a procession. At the right are two panpipers with animal headdresses. In the center are two simply dressed figures carrying rattlepoles with trophy heads at the top; the rattles were probably shells.

5–17. An elaborately dressed man plays a flute. Unlike most Mochica men, this ▷ wrinkled-faced figure is wearing long trousers.

A chapter on Mochica art should include what is known of the performing arts—especially music. Music played a part in Mochica funerary rites, for the representations on grave goods most frequently associate music with the dead. Musical instruments occasionally appear in processions of the living, but these may well represent funeral processions. Not only does the pottery show a variety of musical instruments, but the pots themselves were sometimes whistles or had rattles in a false bottom. Actual instruments have also been found. Panpipes clearly had the highest social status of any of the instruments represented (Ill. 5–16). The fanged deity himself is depicted playing panpipes. In scenes with several musicians, those playing panpipes are larger and more elaborately dressed than the figures with trumpets or other instruments. Six-tubed panpipes were made of clay or cane. Robert Stevenson notes that these panpipes were laid in graves beside the dead as if ready to be played.

5–18. A curved clay trumpet with an animal head on the end. The body markings probably represent those of a snake. Eleven inches long.

5–19. A white-ware figure of a kneeling ▷ warrior. His shield and the mushroom design with Maltese cross over his head are inlaid with a black, tarry substance. He once held in his right hand a club of wood or metal.

There were also flutes (*Ill. 5–17*) and trumpets of several sorts. Conch-shell trumpets were used, and sometimes clay imitations were made of the large conch. There were also clay trumpets in vertical or recurved shapes (*Ill. 5–18*). Many of these end by flaring into an open-mouthed feline head. The recurved types are commonly found as grave goods. The Mochica had two kinds of drums—one held vertically and the other horizontally—that are represented with great frequency on pottery, sometimes played by a human being or a skeletal figure, and sometimes by an animal-headed creature such as a seal (*Ill. 5–15*) or a fox or a hummingbird. Rattlepoles, with shell or metal disks, are depicted infrequently, and were possibly used for processions, but not for grave goods, nor for the use of the dead. The rattlepoles are represented with a human head at the top, which may or may not have been an actual trophy head. It is possible that the rattlepoles are connected with victory celebrations and not with funerary processions.

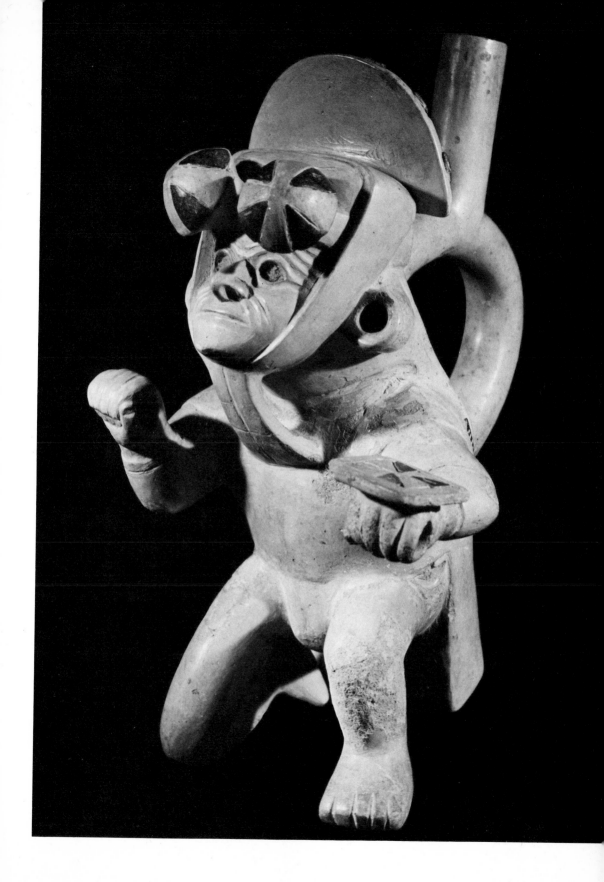

5-20. A black-ware pot with a human or deity head coming out of a bunch of tubers. The headdress and bracelets are inlaid with turquoise.

It should be clear by now that of all the arts and crafts that tell of the Mochica achievement, the pottery is outstanding (*Ill. 5–25*). There were plain wares for everyday, but the decorated pottery, made in notable quantity, quality, and variety, is of particular importance to the student of Mochica civilization and was undoubtedly also of great importance to the Mochica. The quantity of pots does not simply reflect the fact that there are more pots preserved than other kinds of objects because of the conditions controlling preservation. James A. Ford and Gordon R. Willey state that there is little doubt that the pottery was made by a small group of priestly craftsmen, and that there seems to be a connection between political domination and the use of the pottery as cult objects. It would appear from the quantity and some of the types of later Mochica pots that pottery came to have secular value as well as religious significance, and was probably a status symbol as grave goods. Since there are no pottery representations of people making pottery, we are not sure whether men or women were potters. It is likely that they were male craft-specialists.

5-21. A black-ware pot with a design made by cutting out the background behind the monster figure.

5–22. One characteristic Mochica pot shape is that of the stirrup spout attached to a blind-spout "cruet." This one has a painted marsh scene combined with modeled and painted frogs.

5–23. A *florero*, with a painted scene on the inner lip. This is a characteristic late shape.

Mochica potters baked in open-hearth ovens a fine-textured paste, usually tempered with fine-grained sand, producing a well-fired oxidized ware that was slipped. North-coast pottery is generally limited in color. Mochica pottery is classified as white-on-red, red-on-white, and red, white, black (in the late period), but there is a wide variety of earth colors found on the pots, including sometimes ochers, earth pinks, and purples. Occasionally, a Mochica pot has as many as four colors, but this is rare. Almost all Mochica pottery was painted, with the exception of a black ware and a very rare unpainted white ware (*Ill. 5–19*). Sometimes monochrome ware was decorated with inlays of turquoise (*Ill. 5–20*) or a black, tarry substance, or sometimes a copper bracelet was added to the wrist of a black-ware figure.

Methods of decoration—actually, of construction—vary from effigy pots, modeled in the round—in the form of human figures, animals, vegetables, and so on—to surfaces with painted scenes. In between is a type of pot with low-relief friezes or groups of figures in a technique like that of Wedgwood pottery. Often these methods are combined, so that an effigy figure may sit on a vessel with a painted scene, or a low-relief frieze of figures may be painted or bordered with a painted design. In some instances, designs were incised before paint was applied. Occasionally, there is an excised technique employed in which clay was cut away to form a raised design (Ill. 5–21).

The shapes of Mochica pottery are of tremendous variety. The vessels may be globular, cylindrical, rectangular, or in the form of whatever animal or vegetable, raft or house is being represented. Most of the painted scenes and relief scenes are on globular pots. Most commonly a stirrup spout is attached to the body of the vessel, but many have wide, open spouts (Ill. 5–24) or, occasionally, a cylindrical spout with a strap handle. Some globular pots have a blind spout (Ill. 5–22). Some pots are shaped like a carafe with a handle; these often have figures in low relief. There are deep bowls with wide, flanged rims, on which scenes are painted, and there are *floreros* with flaring rims (Ill. 5–23). There are also bowls like dippers, banjo-shaped, with a handle and a hole in the center; these are frequently called "corn-poppers," suggesting what may have been their function. Goblets (uncommon in reality but frequently depicted in painted scenes) are another form. There are also some pots that are whistles or rattles, including double-vessel whistling jars that derive from the earlier Gallinazo style.

Many of the effigy figures and portrait heads were made in molds, although they may ultimately be painted differently or have different spouts. Handles and spouts were molded separately and then attached to the body of the pot. There are instances of two different pots representing a head made from the same mold, but one will have a stirrup spout while the other has a flared spout.

The shapes vary at different periods in Mochica development, and the seriation that has been set up for this pottery by Rafael Larco Hoyle depends to a large extent on the spout forms, although shape, decoration, and subject matter are also important factors. Mochica I stirrup spouts (Ill. 5–26) generally have a thickened lip, reminiscent of the somewhat thickened lip of Chavín spouts. The vessels are rather compact, and the spout is fairly short. Mochica II has a somewhat svelter lip, and its spout tends to be longer (Ill. 5–27). Mochica III has a more flared spout (Ill. 5–28) with a slightly concave outline; this is a period of elegant style and the introduction of new slips. Mochica IV, the longest of these periods and the period of greatest realism and variety in art, as well as the greatest general development and expansion of Mochica culture, has a long, straight-sided, cylindrical spout, without lip (Ill. 5–29). Mochica V is characterized by a stirrup that curves inward at the base so that the bases of the two ends of the stirrup almost meet (Ill. 5–30). The painting style of this period tends to be more florid, sprawling, and decadent. Generally, both the shape and the decoration of the pots develop from the compact to the florid during the development of Mochica pottery.

5-24. A wide-spouted pot representing a standing anthropomorphic owl.

5–25. One of the most beautiful of Mochica portrait vases, with half-painted face and a snake motif on the headdress.

5–26. A Mochica I pot of the moon monster. The compact spout, with thickened lip, is typical of Mochica I. Such highly polished ceramics may have been waxed.

5–27. A Mochica II effigy jaguar, from the Huaca de la Luna. The spout is somewhat longer and the lip less thick than in the Mochica I pots.

5-28. A Mochica III effigy head of the fanged deity, elaborately modeled and painted with particularly skillful craftsmanship. The spout is slightly flared.

That the pots had a sacred function is indicated by their representation on the pottery. They appear in various scenes with the deity—when he is catching a fish, making love, receiving the bean runners, and so on—and in scenes having to do with human sacrifice and in scenes with the dead. Pots represented not only the creatures or events of Mochica myth and belief but must themselves have had a special value and meaning, because they were made as offerings or for ritual use. In spite of their variation in quality, and in spite of the great quantity that was made—often by mass-production methods—they themselves were objects of sacred significance.

5–29. A Mochica IV pot, with a painted scene of the deity as a crab holding a fishing line. The spout is straight-sided.

5–30. A Mochica V pot, with a busy and sketchy scene of bean-runners on the body of the pot and headdresses on the spout. The stirrup has become almost angular, and the two sides come close together at the base.

5–31. An animal head and paws of copper. Similar ornaments are pictured on the headdress of the fanged god, where they usually represent a feline; here the animal is probably a fox. It has danglers and inlaid eyes of shell.

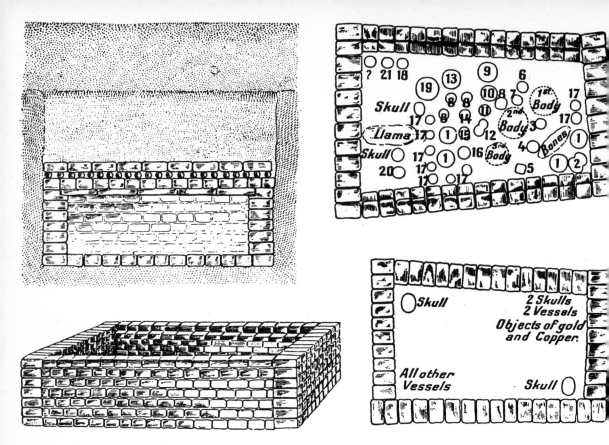

6–1. Drawings of two adobe tombs found at the foot of the Huaca de la Luna, showing the contents of each. The upper had a llama burial as well as three human bodies, two skulls, and miscellaneous bones. The lower contained two skulls and grave goods, but no bodies.

6–2. The Tomb of the Warrior-Priest at Huaca de la Cruz, with the cane lid removed to show the various offerings, particularly pots.

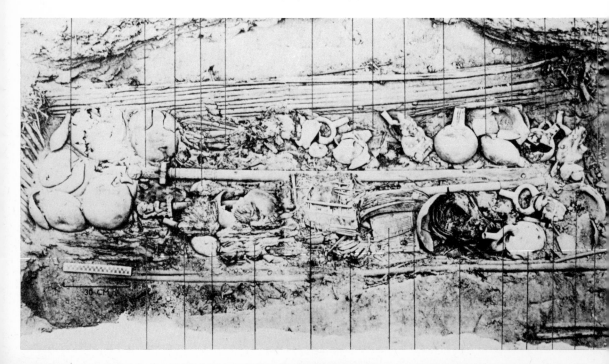

Chapter six

Death And Life

Death cults were common throughout Central Andean history. People clearly believed in an afterlife, and the dead were equipped for it with offerings often, apparently, made specifically for burial. The textiles in mummy bundles that show no signs of wear, the miniature feather shirts that could not possibly have been put on, and the elaborate pottery that has not been used all attest to this practice.

The typical Mochica grave was a rectangular tomb—occasionally with niches for offerings—made of adobe bricks that were sometimes plastered (*Ill. 6–1*). Often cane coffins were used, or the graves were roofed with cane. There were also simpler burials in oval pits. The burials were generally extended, with the head to the west. Cane or algarroba posts were often erected at the head, possibly as grave-markers. It has been suggested that the cane may have been intended to permit the dead to breathe or receive liquid offerings, but, although these canes were placed at the west end of the burial, they were not always directly over the face. Bodies were first wrapped in cloth and then in cane mats. Undecorated gourd bowls were often used as face or head coverings, and, in some graves, copper masks covered the face. A tube or folded plaque of copper, silver, or gold might be wrapped in cotton and placed in the mouth of the dead. Red pigment was sometimes applied to the face or body.

A variety of offerings was placed in the graves. Differences in the elaboration of burial, in the quantity and quality of grave goods, appear to relate to social status rather than to sex or age. Although, judging from the pottery representations, women did not have an important place in the social structure, their burials seem to have been as elaborate as those of men. There are children's burials in simple pit graves, but there are also elaborate children's burials. One of the most impressive burials reported is the Tomb of the Warrior-Priest at the Huaca de la Cruz in the Virú Valley (*Ill. 6–2*). Among the objects it contained were an elaborate wooden digging-stick with a copper blade and multicolored shell and turquoise inlay, representing the deity as the god of agriculture (*Color Plate VII*); a wooden staff with a carved owl-figure; a carved wooden mace or club with a copper point and relief carving of a battle scene surmounted by a modeled bird; a bird headdress of fibers, cloth, and feathers; a mouth mask of gold-plated copper, inset with a polished stone—possibly a mirror—that was surrounded with turquoise beads; a copper face mask, probably originally part of a headdress; a slat box; a feather fan; plumes; a turquoise necklace; a number of pieces of cloth; various objects of copper and gilded copper; and twenty-seven pots. The elaborate digging-stick appears to have been not an object newly made for burial but a treasured antique that had been repaired.

Since almost every field report from Mochica country describes pocked ground where pot-hunters have been at work, it is rare that an untouched grave has been found by archaeologists. It would be helpful in the reconstruction of Mochica thought to have more specific grave associations, to know what kind of pots and other paraphernalia were interred with what kinds of people. In the tombs Max Uhle excavated near the Huaca de la Luna, he found that certain graves seemed to specialize in certain ceramic forms; one tomb had a very high percentage of all the *floreros* found at the site, while another had an unusually large proportion of stirrup-spout pots. William Duncan Strong and Clifford Evans, Jr., suggest that in the Virú Valley there was a possible association between female burials and vessels with one sealed spout. Two burials at the Huaca de la Cruz showed an emphasis on pots representing birds. However, evidence of this kind has not been extensive enough to permit generalizations. An interesting observation made by Strong and Evans is that they found no correlation at the Huaca de la Cruz between tombs with fine metal objects and those with fine pottery; tombs with extraordinary metalwork might have very simple pottery, and tombs with fine pottery might have little or no metalwork.

The deceased himself was probably not depicted on the pottery in his grave. A portrait vase most likely represented the local ruler (*Ill. 6–3*), whose image was put in the grave so that the deceased could go on serving him. Judging from the number of pottery scenes involving the fanged god, it was probably common practice to have a depiction of the deity's activities in one's grave. The Warrior-Priest, who was presumably a leader in political, military, and religious affairs, and possibly the last of the original conquering Mochica lineage in the Virú Valley, had in his tomb three pots with scenes of the deity.

There are many representations of dead people on Mochica pottery. The dead are generally represented with skulls and ribs showing, but with the bodies otherwise fairly normal. There are cruet-shaped or stirrup-spout pots, most frequently in the "Wedgwood" technique (*Ills. 6–5 and 6–6*), depicting friezes of skeletal figures holding hands like children playing a game. These relief figures often wear kilts and sometimes headdresses. There are usually a woman and a child, as well as pairs of panpipers facing each other, and often other musicians with flutes, drums, or rattlepoles. In addition, there are depictions of pots in these scenes, perhaps representing the pots that were put in the tombs. These scenes would seem to represent an afterlife in a happy land with music, dancing, and chicha. In a painted version of this theme, there are stars, suggesting that the dead went to heaven; stars are not depicted, however, in the examples in relief.

6–3. A portrait of a man, probably a chieftain.

6–4. A skeletal figure with the carcass of a deer held around his shoulders.

6–5. A drummer with a diseased face, looking like that of a mummy, sits on top of a "Wedgewood" relief showing a frieze of dead figures with pipers above them and covered pots below.

6–6. A drawing of a pot showing a painted frieze of dead figures surrounded by pots. On top sits a modeled dead couple, the man holding panpipes in one hand and embracing a woman with the other.

The fact that a number of people are shown may signify that several human beings were sacrificed to accompany an important dead person. This theory is evidenced in the Tomb of the Warrior-Priest: There is one burial in the tomb that was probably intrusive at a later time, but, with the Warrior-Priest, there were contemporary burials of two women and a boy. The women were crowded in at each end of the tomb in distorted positions, without wrappings; there was a sash around the neck of one. The boy had a deformed skull and abnormal facial features, but he wore a waistband of plaques of gilded copper. He may have been a page of the Warrior-Priest. The numerous representations of deformed people in Mochica pottery indicates that they had some special significance, and the deformed boy's burial in the Tomb of the Warrior-Priest confirms this.

On top of the afterlife pots, there is frequently a modeled figure playing a drum or panpipes. Effigy pots also represent the dead, and sometimes these figures too play musical instruments. There are also seated skeletons holding animals or animal hides over their shoulders (*Ill. 6–4*). A few pots exist in the form of a skull; at least one of these has the mouth and ear ornaments of the deity, indicating that even the deity could die—although surely he was reborn. Like the relief pots, the modeled dead are generally shown with skulls or "mummified" faces and bony rib cages, yet, unlike the figures in most of the relief scenes, the modeled skeletons do not wear headdresses but rather a plain, hooded cloak. Otherwise, they are nude with a fairly normal depiction of the body, including a live, and often erect, penis.

6–7. A drawing of a relief pot showing the deity in a house making love to a woman. Although the drawing misinterprets certain details—by attaching the rooftree to the headdress, for instance—the jaguar-"sunrise" headdress and the snake belt make it clear that the deity is represented. The lizard helper stands to the right, in front of a house with two women. Anthropomorphic birds are shown to the left.

6–8. A depiction of anal coitus between a man and a woman with painted faces.

6–9. A "family scene" in which the man, in spotted headdress, is having intercourse with the woman, while a child lies in front of her. They lie on a platform with a wave motif.

6–10. A scene of a man and woman copulating.

6–11. A skeletal figure ▷ and a living woman embrace as she holds his phallus. The pots identified with death scenes are painted on the platform at their feet; the cylinder on which they sit is decorated with bands like those frequently depicted on the bases of temples or important houses.

The dead frequently appear on the pottery in scenes of sexual activity (*Ill. 6–19*). These depictions are part of a large corpus of erotic material in Mochica art, in which sexual acts and organs are shown very explicitly. Erotic art in pre-Columbian cultures is rare. There is almost none in Mesoamerica, and it is uncommon in Peru, although examples can be found in other cultures contemporary with, and earlier than, the Mochica (Vicús, Salinar, Gallinazo, Recuay, and Nasca in the south), as well as in the later Chimú. Mochica art offers depictions of coitus, petting, masturbation, fellatio, as well as representations of isolated male and female genitalia and of men and women with exaggerated sex organs.

138

6–13. Two frogs shown copulating. The upper frog seems to be part jaguar and has plants on its back.

6–12. A skeletal man and woman embracing on top of a pot decorated with a wave motif.

6–14. A figure whose head is in the shape of a penis glans. He holds his hands in the "prayer pose" that is often used by deities or demons.

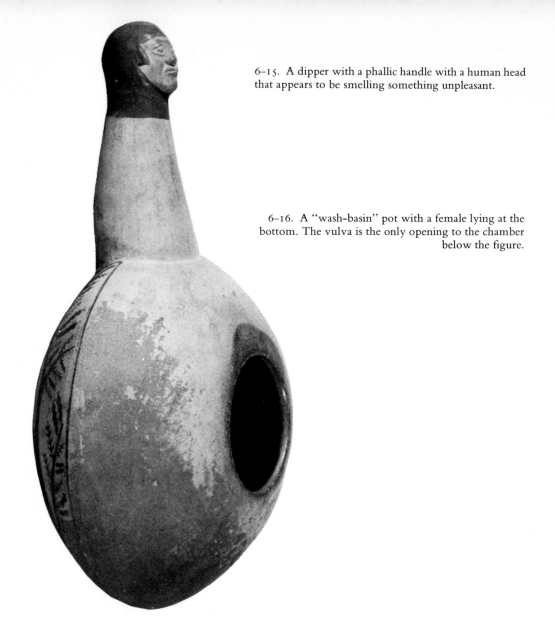

6–15. A dipper with a phallic handle with a human head that appears to be smelling something unpleasant.

6–16. A "wash-basin" pot with a female lying at the bottom. The vulva is the only opening to the chamber below the figure.

Women are rarely depicted in Mochica art. They are probably shown more frequently in sexual activity than in any other kind of scene. There are a few scenes in which the fanged god grasps the hair of a woman with a child wrapped in a shawl on her back and a pot lashed at her waist. The fanged god is unarmed in these scenes, but otherwise the scene is reminiscent of his conflicts with sea monsters. Perhaps he is attacking the same woman with whom he is later shown making love. But who is the child, and why does the woman carry the pot? Pots are usually associated with death. Women appear also in the frieze scenes of the dead, and occasionally in painted scenes having to do with sacrifice. There are a few pots that seem to represent a mother and child (*Ill. 6–21*). However, there are others where the woman is very large and the figure with her does not appear to be a

child, but a very small man who has the haircut associated with prisoners. This woman sometimes has what is undoubtedly a coca bag. She may represent a female deity or demon and her victim; there may have been a legend of a woman who first brought coca from over the mountains and perhaps demanded a victim in return. But otherwise there is no evidence of a female deity. The female is most often a rather ordinary looking woman who is the sex partner of a male.

Paul H. Gebhard has observed that the love-making scenes are modeled in full round rather than painted. Although some subjects in Mochica art appear in all techniques, others are found in one technique rather than another. Sometimes this distinction may simply relate to practical craft limitations—and it is always possible that examples of a missing category may be destroyed or undiscovered or that they exist only in unidentifiable sherds—but there is some indication that there was a correlation between subject matter and technique in several categories of Mochica representation. There is only one erotic subject that appears in low relief, for example: This is the scene showing the fanged god copulating. The copulating deity sometimes appears on three-dimensional pottery, but such representations are less common than elaborate scenes in low relief. The shape of these pots is frequently the same cruet type as those on which death scenes appear in relief. On a number of the pots, the deity, wearing a jaguar headdress, is lying in a house with a woman (*Ill. 6–7*). Outside the door is an anthropomorphic bird who seems to be throwing liquid from a container at the couple. Sometimes the bird is descending a small stepped platform, while another bird stirs something in a pot, and a third flies above. On the other side of the house, several animals, including the lizard helper, watch and wait. In one version of this scene, a small feline waits at the side. In another, intercourse takes place under a tree rather than inside a house; in fact, the tree may be sprouting from the god's belt. In the most common version of the scene, there is a stirrup-spout vessel represented above the woman's head, and a wave motif in a band at the bottom of the pot. The scene seems to relate a myth.

Most of the erotic pottery portrays nondivine human beings, modeled entirely in the round, and the most common type of sexual representation is copulation. This act is depicted in a number of positions (*Ill. 6–10*), some of which are realistic, some of which are physiologically impossible. In many cases, anal coitus is shown (*Ill. 6–8*). The depictions of coitus always involve only two people; there is a group of "family" scenes (*Ill. 6–9*), however, in which a male and a female are copulating, usually under a coverlet, while a child lies beside the mother, often nursing. The coverlet hides the couple discreetly from three angles, but, from the lower view, the sexual activity under the blanket is quite clearly depicted.

In the scenes of coitus generally, kissing is nonexistent, but there is another group of pots on which petting scenes are represented. Whereas copulation almost always takes place between a living woman

6–17. A man seated on a throne, holding an enormous phallus. There is a hole in the phallus. If one attempted to drink or pour from the headdress, he would be sprinkled through the holes in it.

and a living man, petting is often shown with a living woman and a skeletal man, and occasionally the woman is also skeletal (*Ill. 6–12*); in general, however, relatively few women are depicted skeletally. Sometimes the petting couples have their arms around each other, sometimes they are tongue-kissing. In some examples, the woman is holding the male phallus (*Ill. 6–11*), and in some the man has his hand on her chin or tongue or breast. There are also vessels with three people sitting side by side. These can be two females and a male, or one female and two males. The central figure is frequently larger than the other two. Usually two figures are petting while the third is simple touching.

Fellatio, contact between the female mouth and the male sex organ, was one of the common subjects of Mochica erotic pottery. There are, however, no clear-cut examples of cunnilingus. In scenes of fellatio, the male is often considerably larger than the female and is usually seated on a throne while the woman kneels before him or, in some instances, is not even completely represented, so that her torso seems to rise from the ground or the lower step of the throne. The act appears to be a form of tribute to the power of male sexual capacity. Mochica pottery generally emphasizes male virility rather than female fertility. Both Paul H. Gebhard and Rafael Larco Hoyle have pointed out the joylessness and passivity of women in the erotic scenes.

The difference in scale of the figures in the erotic scenes is interesting and inconsistent. It is probably most common to find both figures of the same size, but, in some instances, the male is considerably larger than the female, and, at other times, it is the other way around, the male often in such cases mounted on a large, sphinxlike female.

There are also pottery examples of animals copulating. Frogs (*Ill. 6–13*), rodents, llamas, and felines are depicted, but it is not always clear what animals are represented. In several cases, there appear to be two different species mating. There are very few instances of a human being and an animal embracing; these are not only scarce but difficult to interpret. Among animal sexual representations there are also seated effigy deer with painted lines radiating from the genitals.

Pots depicting isolated genitalia take a variety of forms. There are dippers with painting around the opening to indicate that female genitalia are represented. More frequent is the depiction of male genitalia (*Ill. 6–14*). Sometimes the handle of a dipper (*Ill. 6–15*) or the spout of a pot is a penis, perhaps with a face on it, or the whole pot may be phallic, showing a straightforwardly realistic phallus or an anthropomorphized one. There are a few representations of mountain jars with the penis rising from the center like another peak.

Of the men and women with exaggerated genitalia there are two fairly common forms that, to a moderate eye at least, have a comic element. One is a sort of wash-basin in which lies a relief-modeled nude female (often wearing a necklace and ear ornaments) with outspread legs (*Ill. 6–16*). There is a space below the figure, so that, when liquid goes in or comes out of the pot, it passes through the vulva, the

6–18. A "prisoner" figure with a prominent phallus. In this instance, the end of the ▷
rope is plain, but other examples have the rope ending in a snake head.

only opening in the inner compartment of the vessel. The other form is an effigy male figure—either skeletal or living—whose phallus serves as the spout of the vessel (*Ill. 6–17*). There is also an open spout at the top forming the headdress of the figure, but there is a series of holes around this spout so that, if one were to drink from it, one would be sprinkled with liquid; one is forced to drink from the phallus, implying the act of fellatio. The holes around the top also serve as the dots or circles often found on the headdress of some of the figures engaged in sexual activity. In some of these pots, the male figure is holding his penis, but it is hard to tell whether this is meant to represent masturbation or whether he is supporting or displaying his outsized organ. Another category is that in which the phallus is not exaggerated but simply prominent or erect. Many representations of the dead belong in this group.

The erotic pottery of the Mochica raises many questions. Since everyday life and ceremonial life were so interwoven, it is hard to accept the conclusion that the pottery was made purely as pornography or in simple representation of sexual activity. Since Rafael Larco Hoyle reports finding erotic pots in the graves of children, they would not reflect the sexual career of the individual while he was alive. They may be intended to indicate a life of sexual felicity in the other world, but the question then arises of why skeletal figures are never depicted in coitus. Larco has written that there is a moralizing aspect to these pots and that the skeletal figures are an object lesson on what comes of sexual overindulgence. Yet, if this were true, it would not explain the entire category of erotica. If the Mochica pots have some generalized relation to fertility, as the prominent sexual organs might suggest, why do so many pots show anal coitus? Gebhard has suggested that this may be an artistic convention, so that the female sex organs can be more clearly shown, or that it may indicate a form of contraception. Sexual abstinence during certain agricultural festivities might also be a clue to the significance of the representations. One needs to know much more, not only about Mochica attitudes toward sex, but about Mochica attitudes towards death.

The iconography of these pieces suggests that some symbolic meaning was included in them. Many of the scenes take place on platforms or boxes decorated with motifs that are part of the standard Mochica iconographic repertory: stripes like those depicted on the bases of buildings and temples, wave motifs, and variations of the step motif. Thrones and platforms are frequent, especially in the fellatio scenes, suggesting the sanctity of the power of the enthroned male whose organ is being caressed. The figures engaged in sexual activity are usually garbed with significant accessories. Although the women are usually nude, they often have face paint, frequently in the Maltese-cross motif. They wear ear ornaments like those used by men of distinction, as well as brackets and necklaces. The necklaces are usually represented with a checkerboard or striped design. These necklaces suggest a ritual significance, for the checkerboard motif is associated with sacrificial victims and the taking of coca. The striped

6-19. A skeletal figure with hands beside the phallus.

6–20. A skeletal man petting a woman whose face is painted with a step motif, scrolls above the lips, and the doll-like eyebrows that appear on certain symbolic Mochica figures.

motif, which may be a variation of the checkerboard, or vice versa, is associated with the platforms of important houses and with the garments or accessories of people in ritual acts. One pot represents the fanged god with snake earring and snake belt embracing a figure wearing the haircut associated with sacrificial victims. The men in the erotic scenes are usually dressed, wearing loincloths, headdresses, and frequently a shirt with the step motif. The accoutrements generally indicate people of high station or people ritually adorned.

The representation of the dead in erotic pottery and the association of the erect penis and death give another enigmatic clue to the meaning of these pots. There is a category of Mochica pots representing nude figures of prisoners or sacrificial victims, all of whom have a rope around the neck, and many of whom have prominent penises (*Ill. 6–18*). In a number of these representations, the rope ends in a snake head that is either nibbling on or close to the phallus. In most cases, the snake head closely resembles that of the fanged god's earring. These figures are all still alive, but one has a strong sense that they are awaiting momentary death. Some of them have the haircut associated with prisoners—the tuft of hair by which the prisoner could be held by his captor. The snake head thus seems to indicate that the prisoner was somehow dedicated to the fanged god and that his phallus, as the most vital, virile part of him is being offered to the god. There may enter here the idea that the snake of the fanged god consumes life and is thereby nourished, as the Aztec sun god was fed by human sacrifice. The snake also carries with it, in South American belief, the idea of purification.

The Mochica clearly perpetrated human sacrifice. Sacrifice to accompany the important dead has been mentioned. The pots also depict human sacrifice to the deity or demons. In addition to the mountain-scene and step-wave pots, various other scenes are associated with human sacrifice. The arrival of the radiant god shows naked prisoners with ropes around their necks; the presence of trophy heads in the scenes may indicate the nature of their fate. The fish monster also may have demanded human heads, for he is often seen holding one. Not only decapitation but removal of limbs seems to have been part of certain ceremonies, for hands, feet, and lower leg-joints are depicted, sometimes singly as modeled effigy pots and sometimes in painted sacrifice scenes with ropes tied around them.

In many of the scenes having to do with the dead or with sacrifice, the rope is tied around the necks of pots. The rope does not seem to have any practical purpose: The pots are not tied to anything, and no one holds them. The rope must therefore have had a symbolic meaning related to the rope around the neck of a human prisoner or a llama or deer, or even the feline depictions. The burial pot is perhaps also to be "killed"—strangled by the rope. In other New World cultures, pottery was sometimes smashed or metal objects were crushed when they were placed in graves; the same idea may exist here.

Hanging and strangulation cause erection of the penis. Modern data on decapitation is meager, but it would seem likely that this form of death might also cause an erection. The trophy heads depicted on pottery confirm sacrificial decapitation, and the rope around the neck of one of the women in the Tomb of the Warrior-Priest suggests strangulation. Skulls found in graves at the Huaca de la Luna may have been the result of decapitation. Decapitated heads may have been thrown into the sea as an offering to the fish monster. Animals were apparently also sacrificed by these methods. Decapitated llama heads have been found in burials in the Huaca de la Cruz. Pottery representations of deer show a rope around the neck and a prominent phallus. Hanging itself would have been an unlikely form of death because of the scarcity of large trees and stout wood. But that would still leave the possibilities of strangulation and decapitation. There might well have been a deliberate choice of forms of death that would cause erection, thereby affirming a life-fertility belief even in death: The death of the victim was a life-giving sacrifice to the god. The importance of the human head is reflected in the trophy-head cult that was prevalent throughout Peru; the heads were not necessarily heads taken in battle; they may have been those of sacrificial victims offered to the god as the most important part of a human being.

In one death scene, the victim is tied to a stake or bound with rope and abandoned to vultures. There are scenes in which birds peck at the eyes and genitalia of bound victims. One of these has two modeled figures, with flayed faces, tied to a stake on top of the pot. Below, painted, is a supine figure with stepped design on the cheek, rope around the neck, arms, and legs, a "radiant" penis, and two birds pecking at him. What is particularly interesting about this pot is that in the "sky" there are black dots like those represented in some of the coca-taking ceremonies. This may simply represent a night scene, but it is possible that there is a significance as an astronomical, or at least nocturnal, ceremony.

Many representations of the dead have the step motif on the cheek (*Ill. 6–20*). Rafael Larco Hoyle believed that the stepped cheek on skeletal figures was a sign of punishment and that it indicated flaying of the skin, so that the mandible would remain attached to the skull. However, in the two known possible examples of flayed faces, the entire face dangles, with no sign of the stepped cut. Moreover, the step on the cheek is common on the faces of the dead whether or not they appear in scenes of sexual activity or castigation, if there were any. The step motif throughout Mochica art is a symbol of power, prestige, and authority, whether it indicates that the person himself was important or that he was dedicated to a deity or even to an important person. The deity himself wears a stepped shirt. Important houses have a stepped roofcomb or a step motif repeated on their bases. The creatures who are the servants of the deity, or dedicated to him, have the stepped headdress. The overwhelming evidence is that it indicates distinction, and so it would seem most curious to find that it suddenly stood for castigation in scenes of the dead. It is possible that, because the dead are usually unclad or wear only a simple

6–21. A pot showing a woman carrying a child on her back. The heads are shown with great sculptural beauty, whereas the rest of the figures is only suggested.

hooded cloak, the step motif on the cheek signifies the station that would in life have been exemplified by clothing.

The importance of human death haunts almost all of Mochica art, represented not only by the quantities of objects made for elaborate burial but also the subject matter of these objects. Yet, behind this death cult there must have been the idea of life—the strength of the race, the fertility of human beings, of the land, and of the sea, and the perpetuation of the sun and of the seasonal fresh waters. The Mochica must have believed in the ultimate duality of life and death as necessary opposites and therefore parts of the same basic pattern. But they were complicated people, and their philosophy does not break down as simply as this. Death and procreation were not simply combined, and mysteries are still left. Yet there are clues here that, with energy, insight, and patience, one should be able to use to understand the beliefs that supported the complicated livelihood of the Mochica, beliefs that they themselves held for centuries and that imbued them with the power to achieve one of the greatest of pre-Columbian Andean civilizations.

Plate I. Photo, the author. **Plates II, III.** Private collection. **Plate IV.** Courtesy of the Dumbarton Oaks Collections, Washington, D.C. **Plate V.** Courtesy of the Linden-Museum, Stuttgart; Photo by Didoni. **Plate VI.** Photo, the author. **Plate VII.** Museo Nacional de Antropología y Arqueología, Lima; Photo by Abraham Guillen M.

1–1. Courtesy of the Museum für Völkerkunde, Munich. **1–2, 1–3, 1–4.** Courtesy of the Dumbarton Oaks Collections, Washington, D.C. **1–5, 1–6.** Courtesy of The Metropolitan Museum of Art, New York, Gift of Nathan Cummings, 1966, 1964. **1–7.** Courtesy of The Art Institute of Chicago. **1–8.** Courtesy of the Museum für Völkerkunde, Vienna. Photo by Fritz Mandl. **1–9.** Courtesy of the Field Museum of Natural History, Chicago. **1–10.** Photo, the author. **1–11.** Courtesy of the Field Museum of Natural History, Chicago. **1–12.** Courtesy of the Linden-Museum, Stuttgart; Photo by Didoni. **1–13.** Courtesy of the Museum of the American Indian, Heye Foundation, New York. **1–14.** Courtesy of the Linden-Museum, Stuttgart; Photo by Didoni. **1–15.** Courtesy of the Dumbarton Oaks Collections, Washington, D.C. **1–16.** Courtesy of The Art Institute of Chicago. **1–17.** Courtesy of The Metropolitan Museum of Art, New York, Gift of Nathan Cummings, 1963. **1–18.** Courtesy of the Museum für Völkerkunde, Munich.

2–1. Reproduced from the collections of the Library of Congress, Washington, D.C. After Baessler. **2–2.** Courtesy of The Metropolitan Museum of Art, New York, Gift of Nathan Cummings, 1964. **2–3.** Courtesy of the Linden-Museum, Stuttgart; Photo by Didoni. **2–4.** Courtesy of the Field Museum of Natural History, Chicago. **2–5.** Courtesy of The Metropolitan Museum of Art, New York, Gift of Nathan Cummings, 1964. **2–6.** Courtesy of the British Museum, London. **2–7.** Courtesy of the University Museum, Philadelphia. **2–8.** Courtesy of The Art Institute of Chicago. **2–9.** Courtesy of the Dumbarton Oaks Collections, Washington, D.C. **2–10.** Courtesy of The Art Institute of Chicago. **2–11, 2–12.** Courtesy of the Linden-Museum, Stuttgart; Photo by Didoni. **2–13.** Courtesy of the Museum für Völkerkunde, Munich. **2–14.** Courtesy of The Brooklyn Museum. **2–15.** Courtesy of the Linden-Museum, Stuttgart; Photo by Didoni. **2–16.** Courtesy of the Museum für Völkerkunde, Vienna; Photo by Fritz Mandl. **2–17.** Museo Arqueologico Bruning, Lambayeque,

Peru. **2–18.** Reproduced from the collections of the Library of Congress, Washington, D.C. After Baessler. **2–19.** Courtesy of the Dumbarton Oaks Collections, Washington, D.C. **2–20.** Courtesy of The Metropolitan Museum of Art, New York, Gift of Nathan Cummings, 1963. **2–21.** Courtesy of The Brooklyn Museum. **2–22.** Courtesy of the University Museum, Philadelphia.

3–1. Courtesy of the Museum für Völkerkunde, Munich. **3–2.** Courtesy of The Art Institute of Chicago. **3–3.** Courtesy of the Übersee-Museum, Bremen. **3–4.** Courtesy of the Museum für Völkerkunde, Munich. **3–5.** Courtesy of The Art Institute of Chicago. **3–6.** Courtesy of the Museum of Primitive Art, New York; Photo by Charles Uht. **3–7.** Courtesy of the Rautenstrauch-Joest Museum, Cologne. **3–8.** Courtesy of the Linden-Museum, Stuttgart; Photo by Didoni. **3–9.** Courtesy of the Museum für Völkerkunde, Vienna. **3–10.** Courtesy of The Metropolitan Museum of Art, Gift of Nathan Cummings, 1963. **3–11.** Courtesy of the University Museum, Philadelphia. **3–12, 3–13, 3–14.** Courtesy of The Art Institute of Chicago. **3–15.** Courtesy of the Museum für Völkerkunde, Munich. **3–16, 3–17, 3–18.** Courtesy of the Linden-Museum, Stuttgart; Photo by Didoni. **3–19.** Courtesy of the Museum für Völkerkunde, Munich. **3–20.** Courtesy of The Art Institute of Chicago. **3–21.** Courtesy of the Linden-Museum, Stuttgart; Photo by Didoni. **3–22.** Courtesy of the University Museum, Philadelphia. **3–23.** Museo Nacional de Antropología y Arqueología, Lima. **3–24, 3–25.** Courtesy of the Linden-Museum, Stuttgart; Photo by Didoni. **3–26.** Courtesy of the Museum of the American Indian, Heye Foundation, New York. **3–27.** Courtesy of the Übersee-Museum, Bremen; Photo by Helmut Jäger.

4–1. Photo, the author. **4–2.** Courtesy of The Metropolitan Museum of Art, Gift of Nathan Cummings, 1964. **4–3, 4–4.** Courtesy of the Museum für Völkerkunde, Munich. **4–5.** Courtesy of the Linden-Museum, Stuttgart; Photo by Didoni. **4–6.** Courtesy of the Museum für Völkerkunde und Vorgeschichte, Hamburg. **4–7, 4–8.** Courtesy of the Field Museum of Natural History, Chicago. **4–9.** Courtesy of The Art Institute of Chicago. **4–10.** Photo, the author. **4–11.** Courtesy of the Peabody Museum, Harvard University, Cambridge, Massachusetts. **4–12.** Courtesy of the British Museum, London. **4–13.** Courtesy of The Art Institute of Chicago. **4–14.** Courtesy of the Linden-Museum, Stuttgart; Photo by Didoni. **4–15.** Courtesy of The Art Institute of Chicago. **4–16.** Courtesy of the Linden-Museum, Stuttgart; Photo by Didoni. **4–17.** Courtesy of the Museum für Völkerkunde, Munich. **4–18.** Courtesy of the Peabody Museum, Harvard University, Cambridge, Massachusetts.

5–1. Photo, the author. **5–2.** Courtesy of the Société des Américanistes, Max Uhle, "Die Ruinen von Moche," in *Journal de la Société des Américanistes* (Paris), V, 1913. **5–3, 5–4.** Photo, the author. **5–5.** Courtesy of the Linden-Museum, Stuttgart; Photo by Didoni.

5–6. Courtesy of The Brooklyn Museum. **5–7.** Courtesy of the Linden-Museum, Stuttgart; Photo by Didoni. **5–8.** Courtesy of the British Museum, London. **5–9.** Courtesy of the Übersee-Museum, Bremen; Photo by Helmut Jäger. **5–10.** Courtesy of the Linden-Museum, Stuttgart; Photo by Didoni. **5–11.** Courtesy of the Museum of Primitive Art, New York. **5–12, 5–13.** Courtesy of The Art Institute of Chicago. **5–14.** Courtesy of the British Museum, London. **5–15.** Courtesy of The Art Institute of Chicago. **5–16.** Courtesy of the Museum für Völkerkunde, Munich. **5–17.** Courtesy of the Linden-Museum, Stuttgart; Photo by Didoni. **5–18.** Courtesy of The Art Institute of Chicago. **5–19, 5–20.** Courtesy of the Linden-Museum, Stuttgart; Photo by Didoni. **5–21.** Courtesy of the Museum für Völkerkunde, Munich. **5–22.** Courtesy of The Art Institute of Chicago. **5–23.** Courtesy of the Museum für Völkerkunde, Munich. **5–24.** Courtesy of the Museum für Völkerkunde, Vienna; Photo by Fritz Mandl. **5–25.** Courtesy of The Art Institute of Chicago. **5–26.** Museo Nacional de Antropología y Arqueología, Lima. **5–27, 5–28.** Courtesy of the Linden-Museum, Stuttgart; Photo by Didoni. **5–29.** Courtesy of the Museum für Völkerkunde, Munich. **5–30.** Courtesy of the Übersee-Museum, Bremen; Photo by Helmut Jäger. **5–31.** Courtesy of the Didrichsen Art Museum, Helsinki; Photo by István Rácz.

6–1. Courtesy of the Société des Américanistes, Max Uhle, "Die Ruinen von Moche," in *Journal de la Société des Américanistes* (Paris), V, 1913. **6–2.** Reproduced from Strong and Evans, *Cultural Stratigraphy in the Virú Valley, Northern Peru*, Pl. XXI, courtesy of the Columbian University Press. **6–3.** Courtesy of The Art Institute of Chicago. **6–4, 6–5.** Courtesy of the Linden-Museum, Stuttgart; Photo by Didoni. **6–6, 6–7.** Reproduced from the Collections of the Library of Congress, Washington, D.C. After Baessler. **6–8.** Courtesy of the Art Institute of Chicago. **6–9.** Courtesy of the Linden-Museum, Stuttgart; Photo by Didoni. **6–10.** Courtesy of the Art Institute of Chicago. **6–11.** Courtesy of the Museum of the American Indian, Heye Foundation, New York. **6–12, 6–13, 6–14, 6–15, 6–16, 6–17.** Courtesy of The Art Institute of Chicago. **6–18.** Courtesy of the Übersee-Museum, Bremen; Photo by Helmut Jäger. **6–19.** Courtesy of the Rautenstrauch-Joest Museum, Cologne. **6–20.** Courtesy of The Art Institute of Chicago. **6–21.** Courtesy of the Museum of the American Indian, Heye Foundation, New York.

Bibliography

BADARACCO, AUGUSTÍN J. "El angelote visto por el artista mochica," *Revista del Museo Nacional*, VIII, No. 2, 296–99. Lima, 1939.

BAESSLER, ARTHUR. *Ancient Peruvian Art*, I–III. Berlin–New York, 1902–3.

BENNETT, WENDELL C. "The Archaeology of the Central Andes," in "Handbook of South American Indians," Julian H. Steward, editor, *Bureau of American Ethnology Bulletin* 143, II, 61–147. Washington, D.C., 1946.

—. "Archaeology of the North Coast of Peru: An Account of Exploration and Excavation in Virú and Lambayeque Valleys," *Anthropological Papers of the American Museum of Natural History*, XXXVII, Part 1. New York, 1939.

—. "The Gallinazo Group, Virú Valley, Peru," *Yale University Publications in Anthropology*, No. 43. New Haven, Conn., 1950.

—, and BIRD, JUNIUS B. *Andean Culture History*. 2nd and revised edition. New York, 1964.

BENNYHOFF, J. A. "The Virú Valley Sequence: A Critical Review," *American Antiquity*, XVII, No. 3, 231–49. Salt Lake City, Utah, 1952.

BOLZ, INGEBORG. "Die stilisierte Darstellung des Rochen in der Moche-Kunst," *Ethnologica*, n.s., II, 552–57. Cologne, 1960.

BROECKER, W. S., and KULP, J. L. "Lamont Natural Radiocarbon Measurements IV," *Science*, CXXVI, No. 3287, 1324–34. Washington, D.C., 1957.

BUSHNELL, G. H. S. *Peru*. New York, 1957.

COBO, BERNABÉ. *Historia del nuevo mundo*, I–IV. Seville, 1890–95.

COLLIER, DONALD. "Cultural Chronology and Change as Reflected in the Ceramics of the Virú Valley, Peru," *Fieldiana: Anthropology*, XLIII. Chicago Natural History Museum, Chicago, 1955.

D'HARCOURT, R. and M. *La musique des Incas et ses survivances*. Paris, 1925.

DISSELHOFF, HANS DIETRICH. *Daily Life in Ancient Peru*. New York, 1967.

FORD, JAMES A., and WILLEY, GORDON R. "Surface Survey of the Virú Valley, Peru," *Anthropological Papers of the American Museum of Natural History*, XLIII, Part 1. New York, 1949.

FURST, PETER. "The Olmec Were-Jaguar Motif in the Light of Ethnographic Reality," in *Dumbarton Oaks Conference on the Olmec*, Elizabeth P. Benson, editor, 143–78. Washington, D.C., 1968.

GEBHARD, PAUL. "Sexual Motifs in Prehistoric Peruvian Ceramics," in *Studies in Erotic Art*, Theodore Bowie and Cornelia V. Christenson, editors, pp. 106–69. New York and London, 1970.

GILLIN, JOHN. "Moche, A Peruvian Coastal Community," *Smithsonian Institution Institute of Social Anthropology Publication*, No. 3. Washington, D.C., 1954.

HABERLAND, WOLFGANG. "Some Wooden Figures from Peru in the Hamburg Ethnographical Museum," in *Proceedings of the Thirty-Second International Congress of Americanists*, 1956, 346–52. Copenhagen, 1958.

INFANTES VERA, JUANA G. "Vegetales que los antiguos peruanos usanon para comidas y bedidas, y que se usan actualmente," in *XXXV Congreso International de Americanistas*, 1962, III, 153–68. Mexico, 1964.

JOHNSON, FREDERICK. "Table of Radiocarbon Dates," *American Antiquity*, XVII, No. 1, Part 2. Salt Lake City, Utah, 1951.

KLEIN, OTTO. "La ceramica mochica," *Scientia*, XXXIII, No. 130. Valparaiso, 1967.

KOSOK, PAUL. *Life, Land and Water in Ancient Peru*. New York, 1965.

KROEBER, A. L. "Archaeological Explorations in Peru, Part 1: Ancient Pottery from Trujillo," *Anthropology, Memoirs*, II, No. 1. Field Museum of Natural History, Chicago, 1926.

—. "Archaeological Explorations in Peru, Part 2: The Northern Coast," *Anthropology, Memoirs*, II, No. 2. Field Museum of Natural History, Chicago, 1930.

—. "Peruvian Archaeology in 1942," *Viking Fund Publications in Anthropology*, No. 4. New York, 1944.

—. "The Uhle Pottery Collections from Moche," *University of California Publications in American Archaeology and Ethnology*, XXI, 191–234. Berkeley, Calif., 1925.

KUBLER, GEORGE. "Towards Absolute Time: Guano Archaeology," *Memoirs of the Society for American Archaeology*, No. 4, 29–50. Menasha, Wis., 1948.

KUTSCHER, GERDT. "Ceremonial 'Badminton' in the Ancient Culture of Moche (North Peru)," in *Proceedings of the Thirty-Second International Congress of Americanists*, 1956, 422–32. Copenhagen, 1958.

—. *Chimú, eine altindianische Hochkultur.* Berlin, 1950.

—. "Iconographic Studies as an Aid in the Reconstruction of Early Chimú Civilization," *Transactions of the New York Academy of Sciences*, Series II, XII, No. 6, 194–203. New York, 1950.

—. "Nordperuanische Keramik," *Monumenta Americana I.* Berlin, 1954.

LANNING, EDWARD P. *Peru Before the Incas.* Englewood Cliffs, N.J., 1967.

LARCO HOYLE, RAFAEL. *La ceramica de Vicus.* Lima, 1965.

—. *Chechan: Essay on Erotic Elements in Peruvian Art.* Geneva, 1965.

—. *Cronología arqueológica del norte del Perú.* Geneva, 1965.

—. "A Culture Sequence for the North Coast of Peru," in "Handbook of South American Indians," Julian H. Steward, editor, *Bureau of American Ethnology Bulletin* 143, II, 149–75. Washington, D.C., 1946.

—. *Los Cupisniques.* Lima, 1941.

—. *Los Mochicas*, I and II. Lima, 1938–39.

—. *Los Mochicas.* Lima, 1941.

—. *Peru.* Cleveland and New York, 1966.

LEHMANN, WALTER, and DOERING, HEINRICH. *The Art of Old Peru.* London, 1924.

MIDDENDORF, E. W. "Das Muchik oder die Chimu-Sprache," *Die einheimischen Sprachen Perus*, VI. Leipzig, 1892.

MONTELL, GÖSTA. *Dress and Ornaments in Ancient Peru.* Göteborg, 1929.

MORTIMER, W. GOLDEN. *Peru: History of Coca, the Divine Plant of the Incas.* New York, 1901.

MUELLE, JORGE C. "Chalchalcha," *Revista del Museo Nacional*, V, No. 1, 65–88. Lima, 1936.

NACHTIGALL, HORST. "Indianische Fischer, Feldbauer und Viehzüchter," *Marburger Studien zur Völkerkunde*, II. Berlin, 1966.

OSBORNE, HAROLD. *South American Mythology.* London, 1968.

PROULX, DONALD A. Quoted in "Current Research," *American Antiquity*, XXXIII, No. 3, 422. Washington, D.C., 1968.

RAVINES, ROGGER, and ALVAREZ SAURI, JUAN JOSÉ. "Fechas radiocarbonicas para el Peru," *Arqueólogicas* 11. Museo Nacional de Antropología y Arqueología. Lima, 1967.

ROWE, JOHN HOWLAND. *Chavín Art: An Inquiry into Its Form and Meaning.* The Museum of Primitive Art, New York, 1962.

—. "The Influence of Chavín on Later Styles," in *Dumbarton Oaks Conference on Chavín*, Elizabeth P. Benson, editor, 101–24. Washington, D.C., 1970.

—. "Interpretation of Radiocarbon Measurements on Archaeological Samples from Peru," in *Peruvian Archaeology: Selected Readings*, John Howland Rowe and Dorothy Menzel, editors, 16–30. Palo Alto, Calif. 1967.

—, and MENZEL, DOROTHY. "Introduction," in *Peruvian Archaeology: Selected Readings.* Palo Alto, Calif. 1967.

DELLA SANTA, ELIZABETH. *La collection de vases mochicas des Musées Royaux d'Art et d'Histoire.* Brussels, n.d.

SAWYER, ALAN. *Ancient Peruvian Ceramics: The Nathan Cummings Collection.* The Metropolitan Museum of Art, New York, 1966.

—. *Mastercraftsmen of Ancient Peru.* The Solomon R. Guggenheim Foundation, New York, 1968.

—. *The Nathan Cummings Collection of Ancient Peruvian Art.* The Art Institute of Chicago, 1954.

SCHAEDEL, RICHARD P. "Mochica Murals at Pañamarca," *Archaeology*, IV, No. 3, 145–54. Cambridge, Mass., 1951.

SCHMIDT, MAX. *Kunst und Kultur von Peru.* Berlin, 1929.

SELER, EDUARD. "Archäologische Reise in Süd- und Mittelamerika, 1910/1911," in *Gesammelte Abhanglungen zur Americanischen Sprach- und Altertumskunde*, V, 115–51. Berlin, 1915.

SQUIER, E. GEORGE. *Peru: Incidents of Travel and Exploration in the Land of the Incas.* New York, 1877.

STEVENSON, ROBERT. *Music in Aztec and Inca Territory.* Berkeley and Los Angeles, 1968.

STRONG, WILLIAM DUNCAN, and EVANS, CLIFFORD, JR. "Cultural Stratigraphy in the Virú Valley, Northern Peru," *Columbia Studies in Archaeology and Ethnology*, IV. New York, 1952.

TELLO, JULIO C. "Arte antiguo peruano," *Inca*, II. Lima, 1938.

—. *Chavín.* Revised by Toribio Mejía Xesspe. Lima, 1960.

—. "Wira-Kocha," *Inca*, I, No. 1, 93–320. Lima, 1923.

TOWLE, MARGARET A. "The Ethnobotany of Pre-Columbian Peru," *Viking Fund Publications in Anthropology*, No. 30. New York, 1961.

TRIMBORN, HERMANN. "South Central America and the Andean Civilizations," in *Pre-Columbian American Religions*, 83–146. London, 1968.

UBBELOHDE-DOERING, HEINRICH. *The Art of Ancient Peru.* New York, 1954.

—. *On the Royal Highways of the Inca.* New York, 1967.

UHLE, MAX. "Die Ruinen von Moche," *Journal de la Société des Américanistes*, n.s., X, 95–117. Paris, 1913.

VALCÁRCEL, LUIS E. *Cuadernos de arte antiguo del Peru*, Nos. 1–6. Lima, 1935–38.

WARDWELL, ALLEN. *The Gold of Ancient America.* Museum of Fine Arts, Boston, The Art Institute of Chicago, and the Virginia Museum, 1968.

WILLEY, GORDON R. "Prehistoric Settlement Patterns in the Virú Valley, Peru," *Bureau of American Ethnology, Bulletin 155.* Washington, D.C., 1953.

YACOVLEFF, EUGENIO. "Las falconidas en el arte y en las creencias de los antiguos peruanos," *Revista del Museo Nacional*, I, No. 1, 33–111. Lima, 1932.

—, and HERRERA, F. L. "El mundo vegetal de los antiguos peruanos," *Revista del Museo Nacional*, III, No. 2, 241–322, and IV, No. 1, 29–102. Lima, 1935 and 1939.

ZERRIES, OTTO. "Primitive South America and the West Indies," in *Pre-Columbian American Religions*, 230–316. London, 1968.

Index

Numbers in italic refer to illustrations preceded by chapter number; roman numerals indicate colour plates